HOW TO SET YOUR *Wedding* TO MUSIC

THE *Complete* WEDDING
MUSIC GUIDE AND PLANNER

Barbara Rothstein and Gloria Sklerov

**Andrews McMeel
Publishing**

Kansas City

How to Set Your Wedding to Music

02 03 04 05 06 KWF 10 9 8 7 6 5 4 3 2 1

Library of Congress Cataloging-in-Publication Data

Rothstein, Barbara.
    How to set your wedding to music : the complete wedding music guide and planner / Barbara Rothstein and Gloria Sklerov.
        p. ; cm.
    ISBN 0-7407-2719-2
        1. Wedding music—Bibliography. 2. Wedding music—Handbooks, manuals, etc. 3. Weddings—Planning. I. Sklerov, Gloria. II. Title.

    ML128.W4R68 2002
    781.5'87—dc21   2002020690

Book design by Holly Camerlinck
Illustrations by RoxAnn Van Fleet

Attention: Schools and Businesses

Andrews McMeel books are available at quantity discounts with bulk purchase for educational, business, or sales promotional use. For information, please write to: Special Sales Department, Andrews McMeel Publishing, 4520 Main Street, Kansas City, Missouri 64111.

We wish to thank our families for their unconditional love and support. Thank you, Jerry Sklerov, for always being there for these two computer novices, and for your constant concern, not to mention the many nights of doing without a dinner companion; Kelli and Keith Sklerov, for inspiring the original idea of sharing our knowledge with others who need expert guidance in wedding music planning—a need unmet until now; Karen and Kevin Whitehead, for your valuable editorial and photographic input and advice; and Carolyn and Leslie Rothstein, for your belief in us, and artistic input . . . musical and visual.

CONTENTS

· · · Chapter One · · ·

VISUALIZING YOUR DREAM WEDDING

· · · Chapter Two · · ·

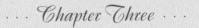

Chapter Three

Chapter Four

Chapter Five

Chapter Six

· · · *Appendix A* · · ·

Appendix B

Appendix C

Appendix D

ACKNOWLEDGMENTS

We would like to thank the many wedding and music experts who shared their knowledge and experience with us so generously. Thanks to Jason Blume for his wonderful encouragement and help in "seeing" the book. We also extend our gratitude to Danno Metoyer of Elite Sound Entertainment for his encouragement and belief in our work; to Mike Carcano of Carcano Entertainment; Joe Farley of DJs to Go; Kemp Harshman, Phil Reyes, John Roberts, and Mark Thomas of the ADJA; Michael Taylor of Hank Lane Entertainment; and Mindy Weiss of Mindy Weiss and Jam, Wedding Coordinators of Beverly Hills.

Special thanks to Randi Rae Treibitz of Randi Rae Entertainment for sharing her expertise and knowledge of the DJ market.

We will always be grateful to Mary Anne Thomas for her tireless support and willingness to help us with her valuable, creative insights.

And we extend our everlasting gratitude to Jason Steele, whose generosity of spirit, artistic talent, and dedication will shine forever on every page.

Letter from a Bride

When Keith and I set the date, all our idyllic dreams of a storybook wedding soon turned into an avalanche of to-do lists. We had to find the location for the wedding and order the flowers. I had to buy my dress, have it fitted, and pick out bridesmaids' dresses. We had to make travel arrangements for our honeymoon, shop for our bridal registry, and on and on. With both of us working full-time, we were pretty overwhelmed.

To my surprise, I found expert help available in almost every area. There were bridal shops all over town with experienced dressmakers. Magazines were filled with wonderful advice and photographs. We even found a local publication devoted exclusively to wedding locations. Wherever I turned, there were florists specializing in weddings, willing to interpret our ideas and add their expertise.

We noticed, however, that there was little or no guidance for music. Luckily for us, that didn't matter because we had Keith's mother, Gloria Sklerov, in our corner. Gloria is a successful songwriter with five Emmy nominations (two Emmys won for wedding songs she wrote for *The Guiding Light* and *Another World*). Based on years of experience in recording songs for film and TV, dealing with musicians, and planning tons of weddings for family and friends, she and Barbara Rothstein, her friend and future cowriter, had devised a system for planning wedding music that truly simplifies what can be a daunting process. Step-by-step, they helped us create a magical wedding, one we felt was perfect largely because of the music planning.

They broke it down for us into simple tasks that we did one by one, and they made the job of planning our music easy and fun. Even though we didn't know anything about wedding music (the only music we listened to was mostly alternative rock—not exactly the best for weddings), we soon began to feel that we knew what we were doing and that our wedding music would be well thought-out and magical.

And it was. Not only did it go smoothly for us, but our guests also had the time of their lives. Practically everyone at the wedding called to tell us what a wonderful time they had and how much they enjoyed the music.

Barbara and Gloria's planning system worked so well, we began to think they ought to share their ideas with other couples. I was thrilled when they decided to publish *How to Set Your Wedding to Music: The Complete Wedding Music Guide and Planner.* I just know that Barbara and Gloria's system will work for you as magically as it did for us. Congratulations and best wishes for a musically perfect wedding.

Kelli Sklerov
Woodland Hills, California

INTRODUCTION

*H*ave you always dreamed of your wedding—the dress you'll be wearing on that wonderful day? Have you visualized the setting—the color of your flowers, your bridesmaids' dresses? When you let your imagination take you to that exciting time, can you hear the sound of the music that will be playing at that very moment?

Now, at last, your dream has come true and you're planning your once-in-a-lifetime day—your wedding day. Imagine the beautiful surroundings you've chosen. Perhaps you plan to be united in a garden setting, under a gazebo draped with romantic antique yellow and lavender roses. Graceful swans float gently on the lake beyond as your family and friends gather in the garden. It's a perfect day.

Or maybe you prefer the warm intimacy of a small home wedding. Whatever the setting, it is only enhanced by the classic and elegant selections of music playing in the background as your guests arrive.

When everyone has been seated and a hush of anticipation fills the room, the sound of a Celtic flute introduces "The Wedding Song (There Is Love)," expressing the spirit and meaning of why you are all there. After this emotional moment, as the procession is about to begin, your guests hear an instrumental version of the magnificent "Aire in G" by Bach. The wedding party begins to walk gracefully down the aisle.

And then . . . it's the moment of your grand entrance—the highlight of the procession and of the wedding. The music is now at the height of emotion, enhancing this breathless moment. For your entrance, perhaps you hear the traditional "Here Comes the Bride" from *Lohengrin* or possibly a dignified orchestration of Pachelbel's "Canon in D." How do you decide? So many possibilities, so little guidance . . . until now. Finally, *How to Set Your Wedding to Music: The Complete Wedding Music Guide and Planner* and companion wedding music CD have been created, especially for you.

We'll help you plan the music for the wedding of your dreams, from your first romantic vision to the very last dance. The guide will encourage you to imagine every nuance and every detail, including the emotions and feelings you'll experience.

HOW THIS BOOK IS ORGANIZED

How to Set Your Wedding to Music contains all the information you'll need, specially designed and organized to lead you step-by-step through a simple systematic process.

Workbook sections follow three easy-to-read chapters that are filled with ideas and fundamentals. Chapter 1 takes you on an imaginary journey through a fairly large wedding to give you an idea of its flow. Chapters 2 and 3 cover the specifics of location, style, bands, and DJs. Indulge your imagination and feel free to read these chapters in any order you wish. Whatever you need to know will probably draw your attention first.

By the time you finish this book, you'll be able to look for locations and interview and audition bands, DJs, and emcees like a pro. (If you have already found a location, you'll understand its musical implications even better.) You'll have a list of the most important questions to ask and an actual preliminary program of your wedding to help you with each interview. You will have created a wish list (Workbook I), refined your program (Workbook II), and completed an actual script for your final program (Workbook III). Even if you have a band or DJ already lined up, the guide will be invaluable in planning your program with them.

The music you select will be one of the most emotional aspects of your wedding, one that you will always remember. From now on, whenever you hear the music you heard as you walked down the aisle or the song you first danced to, you'll be moved again as you remember that beautiful day.

We invite you to make the most of and enjoy every minute of planning and choosing the perfect music for your wedding. Indeed, we're here to help you "Set Your Wedding to Music"!

*Music is love,
in search of its voice.*

Chapter One

VISUALIZING YOUR DREAM WEDDING

isualizing your dream is one of the most important parts of planning, for behind every successful creation is an idea . . . a heart's desire. The clearer your vision, the easier you'll find the process of making it a reality. At the beginning, it's important to allow yourself the time to explore your own personal preferences and consider many different options. Remember—this is a creative process. Let your ideas flow and your natural creativity take flight.

Think of your wedding as a film. Like any successful film, a great wedding has an interesting and meaningful opening and dramatic moments that build in intensity to an exciting climax and satisfying ending. But a great film, though beautifully directed and produced, comes alive only when the composer adds the musical score. The soundtrack is the greatest single influence on the emotion and pacing of a film, just as the music is crucial to the emotion and pacing of a wedding.

Pretend that you are the composer and the music you choose is the soundtrack of your wedding. Make believe that it's the first time you're seeing the "rough cut" of the film you're about to score as we take an imaginary journey through your wedding, scene by scene. Imagine how you'll feel when your family is walking down the aisle, or the moment of your entrance as the bride. Now imagine music that expresses these feelings. "I think the best use of music in a film is when it brings out things that are not necessarily explicit," says Elmer Bernstein, Academy Award–winning film composer. Music can heighten the emotions you'll feel on this meaningful day—emotions that are often difficult to express in words.

BASIC WEDDING TERMINOLOGY

Successful wedding planners, consultants, and musicians instinctively conceptualize different parts of the wedding as scenes, using the following definitions:

Prelude/pre-ceremony: The very beginning of the wedding, the time when the first guests arrive. Often a time for refreshments or cocktails and hors d'oeuvres before the ceremony begins. Sometimes simply the moments before the ceremony when guests have just been seated.

Pre-processional: The time just before the wedding party enters when everyone is gathered together waiting for the procession; includes the time when honored guests who are not part of the official wedding party are escorted down the aisle.

Processional: The entrance of the wedding party and the bride.

Ceremony: The exchange of vows and rings—the time for prayers, blessings, invocations, and pronouncements. (Note that sometimes wedding coordinators/musicians/DJs loosely refer to *all* events that take place before the reception as the ceremony.)

Unity candle: An optional part of the ceremony; usually a candle lighting and brief period of reflection on the uniting of the bride and groom and the joining of two lives (and two families) into one.

Recessional: The joyous post-ceremony return of the bride and groom and the newly joined family down the aisle, followed by the guests' exit.

Interlude/postlude/cocktail or champagne hour: The time immediately after the ceremony and just before the main reception. The time to congratulate the couple formally in a receiving line, or informally while pre-dinner cocktails and hors d'oeuvres are served.

Reception: The time after the ceremony for celebrating. It may feature a sit-down dinner, a buffet, or light refreshments. It's always after the interlude. (Not all weddings have full dinner or dance receptions, but all weddings may be set to music.)

Using these categories when dealing with wedding professionals will not only make communications between you clearer, it will also give you a natural framework in which to build variety and drama.

Imagining Your Dream — Scene by Scene

PRELUDE

The prelude is a beginning, just as your marriage is a beginning. It's appropriate for the music to be somewhat reflective in tone to symbolize this and to allow your family and friends to join and support you emotionally and spiritually. Though your wedding day will be a day of joy and of new beginnings and a celebration of your love, it's also a time for serious reflection on the commitment and vows of a lifetime and the uniting of two people and two families. Sadness may even touch you as you remember loved ones who are no longer here to share in your happiness.

From the minute your first guest arrives, you'll want to establish an atmosphere and mood that captures the feelings and importance of this day. Just as an overture of a musical brings the audience into the world of its characters and prepares it for the opening, the music you've selected for the prelude will gather everyone into your world as you include them in this wonderful new chapter of your life.

Prelude instrumental music can vary from the simple sound of a harp, guitar, or keyboard to the combined sound of keyboard and flute, keyboard and guitar, or keyboard and cello or violin. You can use a string quartet if your tastes run to classical music. This is also a good time to play romantic soundtrack albums, such as *Out of Africa* or *Dangerous Beauty*. These classic instrumentals are perfect background music for an atmosphere filled with emotion and expectation.

Let the music reflect the mood you want to create. If you decide to have a pre-ceremony cocktail hour, a low-key jazz piano or a combination of a piano and guitar or bass would be perfect. Whether your guests are socializing or just sitting quietly, waiting for the wedding to begin, you can't go wrong with a keyboard or a keyboard combination softly playing instrumental ballads. Another possibility for an "upbeat" cocktail hour is to use your favorite songs from "pop" CD soundtrack albums, such as *Sleepless in Seattle* or *My Best Friend's Wedding*, along with instrumental music CDs you particularly like.

PRE-PROCESSIONAL

One of the main purposes of the pre-processional is to allow close family and friends who may not actually be participating in the wedding to be seated first, usually in an honored position. You can use the same selection from the beginning of the pre-processional to the end of the processional, right up to the ceremony, especially if you have a small wedding party. However, if you have a rather large family (or a large wedding party), your processional will be longer. In that case, it's a good idea to have different selections for the pre-processional and processional, not only to distinguish special members of the wedding party, but to add variety.

In some cases, an usher may escort the mother of the bride down the aisle separately so that the bride can be given away by her father. If you decide not to have both parents give you away, this would be a wonderful opportunity to honor your mother, or someone else close to you, by playing a special pre-processional selection as she is escorted down the aisle. Songs such as "You Are

Planning Tip

Unless specifically requested to do so, people generally will not arrive exactly on time. It's important to have music playing as your guests arrive before the ceremony begins. It sets a warm, welcoming tone.

So Beautiful" and "Wind Beneath My Wings" are ideal. This is also the time for accompanying elderly family members and other special people down the aisle to their seats.

PROCESSIONAL

When the first members of your wedding party begin to walk down the aisle, the music should be grand and elegant, just as the word *processional* implies. One of our recommendations is Pachelbel's "Canon in D," with its dignified, measured rhythm.

CDs are great for a musical tour of your wedding. It's fun to just turn up the music and let your imagination take you through each scene. Close your eyes as you listen to other traditional favorites and imagine your family and friends walking with slow, measured steps in time to the music. Then picture them walking in time to more contemporary songs or melodies. And, imagine an adorable little flower girl with a basket of rose petals charming everyone as she walks down the aisle to "Minuet in G" (from Mozart's *Don Giovanni*) just before your entrance.

Electronic keyboards are perfect for the processional. They can easily switch from the quieter prelude and pre-processional music to a bigger sound, adding an assortment of strings, bass, bells, or a harp, all pre-programmed into the instrument. If you're looking for the fuller, richer sound of an orchestral arrangement, CDs are also ideal.

Planning Tip

If you decide to have a pre-ceremony cocktail reception, arrange to have music continue in the cocktail reception area until the last guests have moved on to the ceremony.

Bride's Entrance

The very first sight of you as a bride walking down the aisle in your wedding dress will be one of the single most thrilling moments of your wedding, an emotional highlight for everyone.

Introducing a different piece of music just before your entrance can be very effective. It adds a wonderful dramatic touch. The traditional "Bridal Chorus" from *Lohengrin* is always an appropriate choice. A contemporary new favorite is an instrumental version of "Con Te Partiro." By all means, enjoy this chance to express your own musical preferences and style. The selection that is right for you is the one that moves you, one that you love. You don't have to rush into this decision. Savor these imaginary excursions and you will know in time just what that selection should be.

CEREMONY

Your guests will be rapt with attention as the invocation is given. The purpose of the invocation is to welcome everyone and express the deep meaning of gathering to witness the ceremony. You might want to take this opportunity to play a special song, one that holds deep significance for you. Many couples write their own declarations of love and commitment for their ceremonies. After vows and rings have been exchanged, formal pronouncements of your marriage will be made.

Planning Tip

By now you probably have an idea of the kind of atmosphere you would like to create before the ceremony. It's important to write down all your thoughts in your "Notes and Reminders" sections; details are easy to forget at this busy time.

Limit the number of special songs
for the ceremony to one or two. Try
to have them sung at the beginning or
middle of the ceremony rather than
at the end, when a song might tend to
make the ceremony feel a little long.
An exception may be when you
choose to light a unity candle, which
can be such an uplifting emotional
moment that a song can work beautifully, even though it may be close to
the end of the ceremony.

Unity Candle

After the exchange of rings, many couples participate in a brief candle-lighting ceremony to symbolize their unity. This is an appropriate time for a mid-ceremony song to highlight prayers and moments of reflection as the two of you are joined. Two lighted candles are presented to you both. Using those, together you light a larger, center candle. A warm gesture is to present the smaller extinguished candles to your parents with a rose or small bouquet while a song that has deep personal meaning for you is played. A candle may be lighted for a loved one who is no longer with you. "Wind Beneath My Wings," "One Hand, One Heart" (from the *West Side Story* soundtrack album), and "Coming Home" (from *Set Your Wedding to Music*) are all wonderful choices for this part of the ceremony.

RECESSIONAL

Just after you are pronounced husband and wife, the recessional will begin. You and your family and friends have gone through an enormous range of emotions in this fraction of a lifetime, from excitement and anticipation, even nervousness, to sadness and love. It's time for a release of great joyous energy—time for a celebration. The music should reflect this. The traditional "Wedding March" (from Mendelssohn's *Midsummer Night's Dream*) has the exuberance and tempo that has made it a traditional favorite for many years and is always a wonderful choice. Just as perfect a choice could be "Chapel of Love," with its fun, infectious feeling.

This is also a great time to play a favorite alternative composition or one to honor your family's heritage. Celtic, Greek, Hebrew, Italian, Spanish, and other cultures have marvelous traditional classics and wedding songs that can add a personal and charming touch. If you have a favorite contemporary pop song or if the story of your love has been captured in one that's yours and yours alone, consider this also as a possibility to add your own style to the wedding tradition.

INTERLUDE

After the ceremony, if you decide to have a formal receiving line (an optional choice these days), you'll probably want to serve refreshments or appetizers while you're greeting everyone. Many couples use this time for a private wedding party picture-taking session, especially when the groom hasn't been permitted to see the bride before the ceremony. During the interlude, music will complement the excitement in the air and make the scene come alive for guests who are waiting to congratulate you before the reception. Often the wedding reception is held in the same room in which the ceremony was performed. After the ceremony, while the room is being prepared for dinner and dancing, cocktails and hors d'oeuvres are usually served just outside in an anteroom or lobby.

Planning Tip

Feel free to play two recessionals if your families are of different origins. This is a time for lighthearted fun and celebration, and liberties taken with tradition here will only add to everyone's pleasure and enjoyment.

For this kind of cocktail reception, a mellow jazz combo would be appropriate, if room permits. A bass, piano, and soft drums are a versatile, tried-and-true combination. To allow for conversation, it's best to avoid loud music, but the music can be lively and rhythmic. There are many possibilities here, and if you have strong musical preferences, this is the time to express them and choose what you personally enjoy.

RECEPTION

Whether it's an informal backyard barbecue at the home of a friend, a white-glove sit-down dinner at an elegant restaurant or hotel, or something in between, your reception should be everything you've hoped for—an expression of your love and happiness.

The size of your reception and your own personal style will be determining factors in your musical decision making. If you're planning a smaller party with little or no dancing, you'll likely have your reception dinner or buffet right after the ceremony. If you'd like to celebrate with close family and friends at a small, intimate dinner, you can continue the same style of music played during the interlude. Much more might seem intrusive and really isn't necessary. If you want live music in an intimate setting like this, a harp, guitar, or keyboard playing softly in the background can be very romantic.

Picture the kind of atmosphere you would love to create.

Planning Tip

If you've used an electric keyboard during the prelude and ceremony, you can easily have a contemporary pop or jazz feel for the interlude by adding a saxophone. Playing soft, romantic compositions, sophisticated jazz and quiet rhythms, or a combination of these styles will please many diverse musical tastes. A keyboard is perfect for all of these sounds and styles. CDs are also great here for playing film soundtrack albums or other instrumental music you love.

Your favorite soundtrack albums and CDs would be perfect dinner music. Two albums to consider are *Romeo and Juliet* and *Dangerous Beauty*, both filled with magnificent love themes. For a larger event, where interacting with everyone at once becomes impossible, plan a fuller musical program. Consider having a small dance floor and providing some low-key soft jazz and pop music. Listening to favorite soundtrack albums and CDs of your own will give you many more ideas, in addition to the soundtrack albums listed among our song selections. (See Appendix A.)

Because an average of 175 guests attend each formal wedding (according to *Bride's* magazine), chances are you will be planning a fairly large wedding. In that case, you can set the stage for a marvelous party scene—the most wonderful party of your life. After the ceremony, everyone will be ready to celebrate as they make their way to the reception area, mingling with one another and congratulating family members.

Inviting and rhythmic music should be playing as your guests enter the reception area. The band or a DJ could play slow dances, Latin rhythms, popular favorites, and even smooth swing numbers.

Bride and Groom's Entrance and First Dance

Your grand entrance is your first formal introduction as "Mr. and Mrs.," and the music should reflect this exciting moment. Something upbeat, fun, and rhythmic is called for, such as "We Are Family" (Sister Sledge) or "The Time of My Life" (from the *Dirty Dancing* soundtrack).

After your grand entrance, the music will segue from the up-tempo favorite you've chosen to the song you've selected for your first dance together. If you don't already have *your song*, you'll find many wonderful, popular song choices for your first dance and other special dances listed in Appendix A. The next selection will be another favorite to introduce the wedding party as your emcee invites them to join you on the dance floor.

Family Dances

One of the most emotional family dances is the traditional father-daughter dance. Another special dance, this one for the groom and his mother, usually follows. Two traditional selections for these dances are "Sunrise, Sunset" and "Wind Beneath My Wings," or choose one of your parents' favorites that also has special meaning for you. Recently, however, there have been some exceptional songs written especially for these moments. These fresh new father-daughter and mother-son songs, as well as songs for stepparents, "blended" families, and even mentors, are available at www.weddingmusiccentral.com, where you can hear samples of all these songs and more online.

This would be a lovely time for your mother to dance with your father-in-law, and your father to dance with your mother-in-law. Your sisters and brothers-in-law can then be invited to dance with each other. Playing some of their musical favorites is a wonderful way to celebrate the joining of your two families. You can be sure that the warmth and closeness between you will touch all your guests as they are invited to join you on the dance floor.

Although these are traditional moments, not all of us have both parents in our lives. You may choose instead, depending on your own family situation, to dance with a godparent, a stepparent, or even your mother, sister, or brother. If it's your second marriage, you might want to dance with a son or nephew. And there's nothing wrong with dancing with aunts, uncles, cousins, and so on. Arrange with your bandleader/DJ or emcee to invite family members to the dance floor in any combination that's comfortable for you and your family. While the music is still playing, all your guests should be invited to the floor and even reluctant dancers encouraged to join you.

Ethnic Dances

This is the perfect time to break into a high-energy ethnic or traditional family dance with everyone participating, holding hands, circling and surrounding the bride and groom. Nothing gets everyone of all ages onto a dance floor quicker than a Greek wedding dance, a Hebrew hora (a traditional circle dance), or an Irish jig. Even those who never dance will gather around and actively participate, clapping in time to the music.

One of the sweetest and most heartwarming memories we have is of Gloria's son Keith dancing the hora arm in arm with his ninety-year-old grandmother. His wife, Kelli, joined her grandfather, who spun around in his wheelchair hand in hand with her, surrounded by a revolving circle of family and friends.

Other Dances

In different parts of the country, there are different reception styles. In the Northeast, the usual order of events is to have all family dances, toasts, prayers, and tributes completed before the first course. After that the party gets into high gear. Typically, there will be continuous music throughout the reception and twenty- to thirty-minute dance segments between courses. In the Chicago area, and the Midwest generally, dancing and partying is reserved for after the cake cutting, and these receptions tend to last much longer.

Once toasts have been made, it's time to get the party going. Here's where playing everybody's favorite dance music—from all generations—guarantees a great time for all. Picture your parents and their friends doing "The Twist" or rock and rolling to "Rock Around the Clock," and everyone swing dancing to Glenn Miller's "In the Mood." Young and old alike will join in line dancing to "The Electric Slide," high-stepping to "New York, New York" with party-favor hats and canes, or even jumping into a conga line snaking in and around tables, pulling in everyone who wants to be part of the fun.

It's important to remember that not everyone is part of a couple. Many of your guests will be single, widowed, or divorced. Group dances are an important way to include everyone.

Not only is music the ultimate icebreaker, but it can also be used to enhance and express the ebb and flow of energy and emotion. Just after everyone has been at the height of party mode with the hottest dance numbers, music can mellow out the mood and encourage pleasant dinner conversation, always a welcome break.

Between dinner courses, you can use special songs for warm, sentimental moments and toasts, and for humor and fun. A highlight of a friend's wedding was when he surprised his bride with a hilarious version of "Peggy Sue." Substituting her name, Debby Sue, he actually performed it himself with the band, to everyone's delight. Memories like these live forever.

Family Candle-Lighting Ceremony

Lighting a unity candle has always been a traditional part of the wedding ceremony. Recently, its popularity and significance have grown as more family members are included. A lovely new tradition is a special candle-lighting ceremony for the *reception* where newly joined family members, especially children from previous marriages, can be recognized and warmly acknowledged as part of the new blended family.

At one point during the reception, the lights dim. The bride and groom light one "unity" candle, which can be displayed on a beautifully draped table. Each child or family member to be honored is called to the table one at a time and handed a tapered candle. Everyone lights his or her tapered candle from the unity candle, and when all the candles have been lit, the guests can be asked to form a "circle of love" around the new family.

Another variation is to have a candelabra with an unlit candle in place for each family member to be honored. The lights dim as the bridal couple lights a separate tapered candle and hands it to the first family member called to the table. He or she lights one candle on the candelabra, then hands the "master" candle to the next one called, and the process is repeated.

When all the candles are lit and the family is gathered around the blazing candelabra, a special meaningful song can be played. "Yours, Mine, and Ours" (available at www.weddingmusiccentral.com), written especially for this moment, is a wonderful choice. The family members then dance with each other, exchanging partners.

Cutting the Cake and Other Special Moments

When you hear the infectious rhythm of "Chapel of Love," it's time to cut the cake. Your emcee will invite you to participate in this fun tradition, and your brothers and sisters, maid of honor, and best man can take this time to dedicate special toasts to you. After the cake is served, the groom may surprise you with a beautiful tribute by dedicating a song especially for you that expresses deep, unspoken emotions. Perhaps he's chosen "Because You Loved Me"(from the *Set Your Wedding to Music* CD) or "When I Needed You Most" (from *Yours, Mine, and Ours*). You'll be moved with happiness and appreciation for the love you both feel.

Wonderful moments of music, dancing, and mingling with friends and family fly by. When the emcee announces that it's time

We learned a wonderful tip from top East Coast DJ Randi Rae Treibitz. She has brides and grooms make a list of the first-dance wedding songs played at their parents', brothers' and sisters', and close friends' weddings. Randi plays each of these favorite songs at one point during the reception. This never fails to bring everyone to the dance floor as they relive the emotions of their own weddings. "Every single person in that room should hear something they love at some point during the night," says Randi.

Planning Tips

If you're having a reception with dancing (and especially if you're having a large number of guests), don't save the best for last. It's important to get the party into high gear early on. Play some smooth swing and build up to high-energy dance numbers after your entrance and first dance. If you wait too long to get the party going, guests are likely to leave early, not realizing there's more to come. Have some high-energy dance segments in between courses and alternate them with more mellow music while your guests are dining. Speaking of mellow, even slightly loud music can be very hard on older people, so be sure not to seat them near the speakers. Mention this to the musicians or DJ responsible for setting up the equipment, so that they can let you know approximately where the speakers will be before you make your final seating arrangements.

to throw your bridal bouquet, you will hardly believe that this magical time is drawing to an end. After a lucky friend catches it, the young men may gather around for the tossing of your garter. The groom will playfully remove it with the encouragement of everyone around you. As the crowd watches with delight, you will hear the familiar sound of "Mission: Impossible" or "Simply Irresistible," and all too soon it's time for the last dance.

The Last Dance

As you dance the last dance to a song like Anne Murray's "I Just Fall in Love Again" or Etta James's version of "At Last," the two of you will share the glow and satisfaction of knowing you have planned the perfect program with music that highlighted and expressed fun, laughter, feelings, and love—all the emotions of a wedding to be remembered forever.

A lovely idea for the last dance was suggested to us by John Roberts, a DJ based in the Maryland/D.C./Virginia area, and head of the

American DJ Association (ADJA). He arranges a circle of love around the bride and groom as he plays "Tonight, I Celebrate My Love for You" or "Can You Feel the Love Tonight?" Everyone circles around the bride and groom, moving closer and closer into the circle as they join hands and hearts in wishing their love and prayers for a happy lifetime together.

Possible Song Selections

Songs We Both Love

_____

_____

_____

My Favorites

_____

_____

His Favorites

_____

_____

_____

Our Families' and Friends' Favorites

_____

_____

_____

_____

Ideas

_____

_____

_____

_____

_____

_____

_____

_____

_____

_____

_____

_____

_____

_____

_____

_____

_____

_____

_____

Notes and Reminders

_____

_____

_____

_____

_____

_____

_____

_____

_____

_____

_____

_____

_____

_____

_____

_____

Notes and Reminders

*Lovers hear their song
in the music of the wind.*

Chapter Two

First Things First—
Facts and Fundamentals

There are important fundamentals to be aware of before taking your first step. In this chapter, we'll give you key considerations to keep in mind when designing a preliminary plan for your wedding. For now, sit back, enjoy reading, listen to lots of music, and write down titles of the songs and albums that you love.

Location, Location, Location—Why It's So Important to Your Music Planning

The location of your wedding will be a major factor in your music planning. It's likely to be one of the first decisions you'll make before you even decide on what type of music you want for your wedding. The location itself can give you direction in making musical choices that will further enhance the style and mood of the wedding. For example, a small home in the country might inspire you to choose more romantic, classical music, while a city hotel would lend itself to more sophisticated pop, R&B, and swing. Some wonderful American castles and mansions are available for weddings in many parts of the country and would be perfect backgrounds for baroque or renaissance music and string quartets.

A location may also limit and narrow your choices depending on the resources available and the nature of the site (for example, a church or an outdoor setting). If you've already picked out a location and then discover it's more difficult to deal with than you originally thought, remember there are always ways to work out a beautiful music program no matter what limitations you find. The key is to be aware of what those limitations are and to work around them.

Use your location to maximize its advantages and minimize its disadvantages. For example, if you have your heart set on being married by the ocean on a beautiful morning, an advantage would be the simplicity of the beach. Play up this natural advantage by keeping your planning simple. Let the ocean sand and sky be one of the main attractions; no need to deal with bands, DJs, or dance programs. A portable CD player and spare batteries may be the only equipment you'll need. Your choices for live soloists would be limited as well. String instruments are incompatible with sand and humidity; therefore, for practical purposes, that would rule out the violin, harp, cello, and string quartet. (Generally, solo string instruments sound best indoors. If your heart is set on live music *and* the beach, your best bet would be an acoustical guitar if the number of guests you're having is small. You can read more about acoustic considerations in the next section.)

If a full live band and/or DJ and dance floor are what you really want, the beach would be a great disadvantage unless you were prepared to go to more elaborate and expensive lengths, such as renting a tent and dance floor with professional equipment, electric generators, and so on.

Another example of simplicity would be the traditional and popular church wedding. Many couples have their wedding ceremony in a church or temple and their reception elsewhere. (Some clergy will not perform the marriage ceremony in a commercial establishment.) Most of the time, the church will provide its own organist and/or choir and a built-in music program. Aside from one or two special pieces you might want their musician to play, all you need to be concerned about is the location and music you'd like for the reception. However, if you don't care for their selections or instrumentation (and not everyone loves church organ or trumpet sounds), you might want to check well in advance to see how flexible they'll be about substituting other music, instruments, and/or CDs.

SPOTTING THE MUSICAL PITFALLS OF A LOCATION

ACOUSTICS

Outdoor settings can be very difficult acoustically. Live microphones can pick up the slightest sound and amplify it so that if a strong wind starts blowing, the sound will come roaring through the speakers, not only drowning out the music and the words of the ceremony but also destroying the ambience you have so lovingly planned.

While the crashing of waves and an ocean breeze can be romantic, these sounds usually interfere with the music. An acoustical guitar is very difficult to hear in this setting unless you have a very small group of people (fifteen to twenty) close to the performer. A quiet lake or lagoon would be easier to deal with acoustically, and it would still provide the romance of the natural setting you're looking for. There are many hotels and inns with beautiful gardens overlooking small lakes that would be perfect. Check out your local yellow pages or bridal shows.

One wedding we attended was on a lavish catering yacht. The music chosen for the ceremony was a flute and an acoustical guitar—a lovely, tasteful combination. Unfortunately, the music was completely drowned out by the relentless droning of the ship's engines, which had to be kept running to cool the air on that hot, humid day. The bride never knew when to make her appearance because she couldn't hear the music signaling her entrance. The guests barely heard the ceremony. It's hard to believe how much planning and organizing went into this unlucky affair, down to the last detail—except for the acoustics.

Large cathedrals and temples are traditional choices for weddings. However, if you want to have an intimate ceremony with special songs or instruments, be sure to check out the acoustics when the facility is empty to be sure that the sound won't be lost in the echo of that giant space. Walk around through different seats and rows to get an idea of the way sound travels in all parts of the room, and, if you can, visit the site when it's being used for an event about the size of yours.

Once you've identified the acoustical problems of a site, you can usually overcome them by planning accordingly and being prepared in advance. Discuss them thoroughly with the staff at the location and those who will be involved with the sound and equipment.

SIZE AND SETTING

Size and setting must also be considered when making choices: A jazz ensemble may be perfect in a large catering hall but a disaster in your living room. Conversely, the sound of an acoustical guitar or harp could be lost in a large banquet hall or cathedral but perfect in a small sheltered garden. Larger rooms call for either a live band, a DJ with a full range of equipment, or your own CDs played with adequate speakers and microphones.

One couple loved dance music and wanted a big-band sound. They hired a ten-piece band and held the wedding reception in a beautiful hotel. The room was perfect for seventy-five to a hundred guests, but unfortunately the music overwhelmed everyone at the reception. While this was terrific for a few wonderful dance numbers the couple's young friends enjoyed, the music was so loud throughout the entire evening that the guests found it impossible to talk to each other. Many politely ate their dinner and left before dessert.

If you want to have a large band, especially one with a huge horn section, make sure you have a large room, filled with at least 150 to 175 people. The size of a location is not as critical with a DJ, whose equipment is easily adapted to almost any size room or outdoor situation and can provide the sound of a big band at a volume just right for the room.

A setting can inspire you with wonderful ideas. A California couple we knew held a fabulous luau for their wedding in Hawaii. They featured Hawaiian music and used the classic "Hawaiian Wedding Song" for their processional. The romantic glow of moonlight reflecting on the ocean in the distance was a perfect setting for the music. Everyone wore traditional muumuus and Hawaiian sarongs and the guests received beautiful, fragrant leis as they arrived. The couple played traditional Hawaiian songs (featuring a few from Don Ho albums), but most of the evening was filled with their favorite pop and jazz selections from their own CDs.

Sedona, Arizona, has been the setting for many beautiful weddings. The sun setting behind the great red rock formations is a breathtaking sight. There, one couple read poetry with the sound of traditional Native American chants and other New Age albums in the background. For the reception at the magical Enchantment Hotel nestled in a magnificent canyon, a four-piece band played a variety of eclectic dance and pop music.

ELECTRICITY AND PROPS—
BASIC EQUIPMENT

Sources of electricity and lighting are crucial considerations. Not only will lighting be important for the room itself, it will be necessary for musicians to read the music and for DJs and emcees to see the program and the script they are to follow. An advantage of using locations that specialize in weddings is that there are rarely any electrical problems. Hotels and catering halls are almost always equipped with props such as platforms and stages for bands, dance floors, tables for displays, backdrops, sound buffers, and even podiums for DJs. But never take anything for granted—always ask.

Your location may not be a professionally equipped catering hall or hotel. In this case, if a friend who is not accustomed to performing at weddings will be providing the music or acting as DJ/emcee, he or she may not be prepared for every contingency. Therefore, designate someone you can rely on, such as a friend or relative *not* in the immediate wedding party, to coordinate with the musicians and/or DJ for:

1. Chairs for all musicians

2. Music stands and lights

3. A few heavy-duty, extra-long extension cords

Planning Tip

Remember to position the musicians or DJ (or whoever is playing the music) where they can easily see the processional so they can pace the music properly and change selections when appropriate.

4. A power strip (six outlets in one)
5. Corded and cordless microphones
6. Speakers (two)

REGULATIONS AND RESTRICTIONS

Different locations have different rules and regulations that will affect your music planning. Some churches and synagogues may have regulations regarding the use of outside musicians and instruments. They may prefer that couples use their choir and organist or other instrumentalist and play only liturgical or traditional music. Be sure to discuss these policy issues with the staff or officials of the church or synagogue you are considering.

Zoning laws and city ordinances can sometimes be stumbling blocks. Many mansions in residential areas have been made available for weddings, but more often than not, the music must stop at a certain time, even if the party is in full swing. The same restrictions may apply at some public parks and beaches, in which case music will not be permitted past certain hours—often no later than ten or eleven P.M. On the other hand, at most hotels or catering halls, the music can go on for as long as you have the right to the room.

Another consideration is the difficulty of getting the equipment to the location. Most bands will charge cartage for locations that are difficult to access. Cartage services specialize in getting heavy equipment to stages, sound studios, and up stairs to the area set aside for musical equipment at each location. Be prepared to pay an extra $100 and up for difficult locations. Of course, ramp access is even more important for handicapped guests.

WEATHER CONSIDERATIONS

Obviously, weather is an important factor to consider when planning an outdoor wedding. If you are having a group of musicians and/or a DJ, you'll have to provide a sheltered area for them in case of rain, direct sunlight, or extreme heat. This is required by contract in many cases, not only to protect the musicians and DJs themselves but also their instruments and equipment. Think of your guests, too, and where they will be sitting during what may be an hour-long ceremony on a hot, sunny day. A contingency plan is always a good idea, and canopies, tents, and even an alternate room indoors should be available.

In colder climates, during the winter months, road conditions should be considered. Discuss the importance of leaving enough travel time in the event of inclement weather with your bandleader, DJ, or emcee so you won't have to delay your ceremony or waste valuable time, nervously waiting for him or her to arrive.

Checking outdoor sites at the same time of day your wedding will be held is especially important. For example, the beach may be calm and still in the mornings, only to give way to strong wind conditions by four o'clock in the afternoon. Generally, however, there is nothing consistent about the weather; it's always unpredictable.

This information isn't meant to discourage you from having your wedding outdoors. On a beautiful day or evening, there's nothing like an outdoor wedding ceremony. However, as with all locations, it's important to be aware of the problems that might crop up later so you can find solutions for them beforehand.

A careful consideration of these fundamentals will guide you in choosing the perfect location for you. First, find the most wonderful setting you can find. When you think you've found it, put yourself in the picture and imagine yourself walking down the aisle at your own wedding. If you're sure it's the perfect place, then think about the practical considerations, especially with regard to the music. If possible, think of these things before you sign on the dotted line for your location.

CREATING STYLE—
LETTING "YOU"
SHINE THROUGH

Style is something that's hard to put your finger on. Some people refer to it as that "je ne sais quois" quality—"I don't know what it is, but it's got that certain something." Style is simply a reflection of all your choices put together. It's how much of you is expressed in your choices.

Think of the kind of music you really love. If you're classical music lovers, you can have your favorites played by a harpist or string quartet to set a quiet, elegant tone before the ceremony. If one of you loves classical music and the other loves jazz, you can have the best of both worlds:

Planning Tip

When you're looking for your location, use the "Location Checklist" on page 37 to fill in as many details as you can about each one in the "Notes and Reminders" sections at the end of this chapter. Remember to write down the name of the person(s) you speak to at each place and any important information you're given. Make sure you clarify everything he or she tells you so there are no misunderstandings later. It's easy to lose track of who said what when you're contacting and discussing details with so many different people. At each location, make a note of the different rooms and areas available for different parts of the wedding and where they are. Is the reception area adjacent to the ceremonial area? Can the music be heard equally well in both places? Often you can use the same player and equipment for a natural, graceful transition from the pre-ceremony cocktail reception to the ceremony, and even the next phase of the wedding.

Have a keyboard and bass combo play sophisticated jazz after the ceremony as a background for a cocktail reception just before dinner. The combination of classical and jazz will reflect your own individual personalities and add a flair and style that's all your own. Of course, other combinations of instruments and musical styles can work just as well. If you decide to have both classical music and jazz, there's still a place for dance music at the reception, where you can express your trendier tastes for pop or more unusual music for dancing and special moments. This is easily accomplished. Good DJs have fabulous collections of CDs—including instrumentals featuring piano and flute, harp and guitar, and other combinations of instruments, as well as all musical *styles*, from jazz to classical. You can also take advantage of a whole range of CDs with a live band, since most bands today provide CD equipment. The band-DJ combination is more and more popular these days, and you might consider going this route, depending on your budget.

Your individuality, personalities, and family backgrounds can all be honored and expressed through your musical choices. Ethnic musical compositions are marvelous as processionals, recessionals, and even special moments during the ceremony. Many couples of different backgrounds use a theme song from each of their cultures or religions at some point during the wedding. This adds a wonderful touch of warmth, family unity, and, of course, style.

One young couple of Russian descent successfully incorporated a live klezmer band in their prelude and processional and used a DJ for the main reception—a great combination of new and old. Their wedding was loaded with style mainly because expressing who they were was one of their main objectives. Because they are both singer-songwriters and wanted to share their work with their family and friends, they recorded five or six original songs and presented them in a beautiful CD favor to everyone at the wedding. In addition, the groom, an aspiring filmmaker-comic as well, directed himself, his bride, and their parents in a hilarious filmed portrait of themselves (à la Woody Allen) that had everyone roaring with laughter. The guests had such a marvelous time that when the wedding was over, no one wanted to leave or say good-bye to that wonderful couple.

Don't be intimidated by rules or others' opinions. While it's good to listen and learn and keep an open mind, you can still express your own style and taste. If you'd like to hire a jazz pianist, consider playing a classical favorite or two in a jazz arrangement. A string quartet would lend an unusual twist to a few contemporary music selections in addition to the more formal classical selections you'd expect to hear. If you love something, go for it! If you're making arrangements for live music, consult with your musicians about unusual choices. Chances are, good musicians will agree to play only what feels and sounds right for their instruments. Also remember that all styles and moods can be achieved with selections played on CDs alone.

SETTING THE MOOD WITH INSTRUMENTS

The art of combining instruments is what professional musicians call *instrumentation*. Instruments create the actual sounds you hear. Each instrument or combination of instruments has its own unique sound and can evoke different emotions and feelings.

Almost any instrument can be played solo, such as a harp, organ, violin, or piano. Some instruments have a wider range of styles and can create many different moods. A blues or rock guitar can lend an urban, contemporary tone, while a classical guitar can provide a softer, quieter one. Flutes have an ethereal quality that can lighten the somberness of a cello or add a carefree or wistful touch to a keyboard, depending on the melody or composition. Each different soloist or combination can set an entirely different mood.

One of the most versatile instruments is the portable keyboard synthesizer, which can be programmed to add bass, rhythm, and beautiful string sounds. It is perfectly suited for jazz, classical, and popular hits of all styles. An instrument of many moods, it can be made to sound as delicate as a harp or as full and rich as an orchestra.

Vocalists, choirs, and gospel and pop singers can also create a totally different ambience according to the material they perform. Songs have moods of their own depending on the lyrics and melody. Some are more versatile than others and do not have to be played as originally orchestrated to be effective. For example, "Can You Feel the Love Tonight?" can be sung a capella (without musical accompaniment) and can be as emotional as a full recorded arrangement, whereas "Livin' la Vida Loca" needs a Latin rhythm (and maybe Ricky Martin) to come alive!

Instruments should be compatible with the kind of music selections you choose—the more suitable the composition or song is to the instrument, the more pleasing it will be to the ear. A harp is wonderful for classical compositions and tender ballads or folk songs but is not geared for hot dance tunes. Chances are, you won't find many violinists playing "YMCA." When the musical selections are appropriate to the player's style and instrument, the music will have a natural and easy-flowing quality.

POPULAR INSTRUMENTS AND COMBINATIONS TO SET THE MOOD YOU WANT

Excellent choices for prelude, ceremony, and interlude:

Harp—gentle, quiet, and elegant

Guitar—slightly warmer, more versatile

Keyboard/piano solo—classic, elegant, universally loved, versatile—good for almost all musical styles

Keyboard and flute—elegant, good for classical compositions, light

String quartet (two violins, viola, cello)—classical, elegant, refined, subdued tone

Flute trio (flute, violin, cello)—lighter than string quartet

Excellent choices for before and after the ceremony, as well as the reception:

Keyboard synthesizer—can be programmed for strings, rhythm, and so on, to change the pace before and after the ceremony to create the ambience you want

Jazz trio—different combinations:

Piano, bass, guitar—soft, smooth, sophisticated

Piano, bass, saxophone—jazzier, more sophisticated, upbeat

Piano, bass, drums—dance, rhythm-oriented, jazz, pop, R&B, upbeat tone, contemporary; can be toned down for pre-ceremony

Excellent choices for the reception:

Jazz trios—choose quieter, smoother combinations for versatility and a sophisticated, elegant, warm atmosphere; can alternate with a DJ for dance music (band-DJ combination)

Variety band (piano, bass, guitar, drums, vocalist)—festive, fun, exciting, and versatile

Swing band (piano, saxophone, trumpet, drums, bass, trombone, vocalist)—full orchestration for a very large dance reception; festive, exciting

VARIETY IS THE SPICE OF LIFE—AND WEDDINGS!

It can be very effective when one or two styles and instruments are used for different parts of the wedding. For example, in the formal West Coast wedding program sample in chapter 6 (page 117), you'll notice that the prelude/cocktail hour, pre-processional, and processional were all slightly different in their musical concept. The soft, tasteful combination of keyboard and flute was used from the time guests first arrived until the ceremony was about to begin, and later on, a keyboard, saxophone, and guitar played soft jazz during the cocktail hour.

Just before the processional was about to begin, an emotional atmosphere of expectation was created by the ethereal, Celtic version of "The Wedding Song." Then, as the bridal party walked down the aisle, the beautiful "Canon in D" by Pachelbel further heightened the emotion building up to the bride's entrance. The contrast between the intimate "Wedding Song" and the classic, stately Pachelbel was as inspiring as it was beautiful. (Both of these new productions are available in the CD *Set Your Wedding to Music*.) For the reception, a DJ, playing fabulous dance music, was used where the couple wanted the mood to be "Let's all celebrate and have a good time."

If you decide on live music, almost all bands come equipped with CD players to accommodate your requests for the specific artists, instrumentals, and original recordings you love. They should be able to play the special songs or recordings you want any time during the wedding. Again, don't assume this; ask them and make sure it's prearranged, including the CDs and/or selections you want played.

A change of pace is as important during the reception itself as it is between different parts of the wedding. There should be plenty of dance segments interspersed with other more emotional moments that are highlighted by ballads and carefully selected, meaningful songs. A complete program of up-tempo loud dance music gets old pretty fast, as would one of all low-key, slow ballads. Remember that you'll probably be having guests of all ages. When making particular music selections for the reception, we would encourage you to play selections from traditional foxtrots to contemporary dance music, from country and rock for line dancing to big-band swing, from Latin cha-chas and mambos to the twist. The greater the variety, the more people there will be on the dance floor having a wonderful, memorable time.

Changes of pace like those described above will make your wedding more exciting. What fun for guests to hear contrasts like Pachelbel's "Canon" at the ceremony and "Chapel of Love" at the cake cutting. Through thoughtful consideration of your musical program, the music can reflect and heighten the feelings you want to make others aware of during the program.

LOCATION CHECKLIST

Use this checklist when you're looking for locations. Keep track of the information you gather at each location for the ceremony as well as the reception. Write everything down when you're there or right after you leave; it's much too easy to confuse one place with another. The guide is handy to keep in your purse or glove compartment so you can always refer to it or write in it when you're out shopping and interviewing for the wedding.

- Address
- Fees and terms
- Ambience
- Type of layout/floor plan
- Room(s) available?

- Phone
- Outside music allowed?
- Acoustics
- Electricity and props
- Catering packages available?

- Contact
- First impression
- Size and setting
- Restrictions and regulations

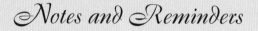

Notes and Reminders

CEREMONY

_____
_____
_____
_____
_____
_____
_____
_____
_____
_____
_____
_____
_____
_____
_____
_____
_____
_____

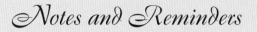

Notes and Reminders

RECEPTION

_____

_____

_____

_____

_____

_____

_____

_____

_____

_____

_____

_____

_____

_____

_____

_____

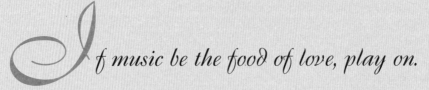 f music be the food of love, play on.

Shakespeare, *Twelfth Night*

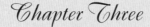

Chapter Three

All You Need to Know About Bands and DJs . . . and What to Ask

When to Look and When to Book

Believe it or not, a year or eighteen months in advance is pretty standard for booking bands and DJs. Remember that the best ones are also being booked for bar mitzvahs, bat mitzvahs, anniversaries, birthdays, and corporate events, often a year or two in advance. If you know your date, look now. If you know your date and location, look and book! Agencies will tell you that it's much easier when you have an eighteen-month advance time, especially if you plan to be married during a busy holiday, such as the Christmas season or Valentine's Day, or in June, one of the busiest months for weddings.

Of course, not everyone can possibly book that far in advance. You might be getting married in four months or less. It's still possible that the musicians or DJs of your choice, and others of the highest caliber, just might have an opening on your day.

Before going on to a fuller discussion of bands and DJs, it will be helpful to compare the key points listed below. This list is designed to give you an overview that will make the information easy to read and remember.

BANDS VS. DJS—KEY POINTS

DJs

- Less formal
- Can provide group dance instruction and live entertainment/interaction with guests
- All recorded music with original artists available
- Sound levels of music easily adjusted
- True continuous music—no breaks
- Great sound systems
- Minimal space needed
- Trained emcee and coordinator
- No tips required
- Less expensive—Smaller cities: minimum of $595–$800 for four hours and up

  Larger cities: minimum of $1,000–$1,500 for four hours and up

Bands

- Brilliant live sound
- Elegant/formal
- Can learn special material not available on CDs or sheet music
- Can spontaneously accompany guest performances
- Limited variety of styles
- Take breaks
- May not provide skilled emcee
- Require more space
- Smaller cities: four- to six-piece band minimum $1,500–$4,000 for four hours and up

  Larger cities: $2,000–$5,000 for four hours and up

  (Price increases with each musician.)

THE MAGIC OF LIVE MUSIC

There's something very special about having a live musician or band play at your wedding. This day is the most important day of your lives and it deserves special treatment. Consider live music, if only for an hour or two for the ceremony and cocktail hour.

WHERE TO START

If you're wondering where and how to find a band and whether live music fits within your budget, a few telephone calls will get you started and should confirm the range of fees in your area. Friends who've recently been married are a good first source of information, contacts, and suggestions. Wedding consultants, photographers, videographers, and caterers all work with musicians and probably would have some great recommendations. Don't forget the place where you're having the reception. More often than not, they have lots of ideas and contacts. Naturally, if you've attended a wedding or an affair recently and particularly liked the music, find out who the musicians were and contact them directly. Soon you'll be ready to shop and compare using the guide's worksheets to keep a record of prices and packages offered by those you interview.

You might also make direct contact with musicians at local bridal shows. These shows are held periodically throughout the year in all midsize and larger cities. It's a fun place to personally meet bandleaders and DJs and see their videotapes. They may even give you sample CDs or cassettes.

Bridal shows are a great place to start. You might feel overwhelmed with all the information "coming at you" at once, but if you take your time and keep all the cards, samples, brochures, and information you receive in one place, you can digest it all at your own pace after the show. Go with the intention of enjoying yourself and being open to all ideas. In most cases, we advise you not to decide right then and there. It's best to wait until you've shopped around a little and had time to think and compare. If you feel pressured by *any* salesperson into making a decision, that's a good time *not* to decide!

For classical musicians, a good lead is a local symphony orchestra. Chances are, many of these professionals are accustomed to playing at weddings. You can also find musicians through the local chapter of the American Federation of Musicians (national offices in Los Angeles and New York, 800-237-0988; 212-869-1330), entertainment agencies, music schools, and college music departments. (Your safest bet there would be to contact a music professor rather than a student. A student may not be as experienced with the timing and sequence of wedding events, as familiar with wedding music standards, or as reliable as a more mature professor or music professional.) You can find school and agency listings in the yellow pages and on the Internet. By the time you have followed up on one or two leads, you'll probably have more than you need.

WHAT WILL A BAND COST?

Generally four players will charge anywhere from $1,500 to $4,500 for four hours. A six-piece band in New York City or Los Angeles might generally run closer to $4,500 and range as high or higher than $7,000, depending on how well known the band is. Fees can be much higher for top talent or name bands and singers. For some celebrity and society bands, the sky's the limit. In smaller cities, the range may be considerably lower, starting as low as $1,000 up to $4,000 or more for a four-piece band. Naturally, the more players there are, the higher the cost of the band. One player, such as a harpist, guitarist, or keyboardist, may be available for a couple of hours for anywhere from $200 to $350 or more.

DIRECT CONTACT VS. AGENCY

If you know some musicians personally, you can deal with them directly. If not, an established agency or music services company can be very helpful in making arrangements and dealing with financial matters and contracts, especially if you are using different musicians or groups of musicians for different parts of the wedding. Another advantage of using a good agency is that they may have extensive experience in planning and dealing with weddings. Bear in mind that the agency will have to tack on a fee of approximately 10 percent to 20 percent in addition to the cost of the musicians. When selecting and using an agency, the same care should go into checking out their reliability and the quality of their musicians as into checking out musicians you choose directly.

WHEN YOU DEAL WITH A BAND DIRECTLY

If and when you decide to book a band, a deposit ranging from 20 percent to 50 percent will generally be required to secure the band for a particular date. Try to negotiate a 20 percent deposit, especially when a band costing thousands of dollars has a policy of forfeitures for cancellations, even months in advance. In most cases, the balance may actually be due five days to a week *before* the wedding, although some bands might agree to be paid right after the wedding. Be prepared in almost all cases to pay by cash or certified cashier's check. Overtime charges are usually paid in cash right after the wedding as well. The hassle-free way is to deal with the most reliable bands and pay them in full a week or so in advance so that you won't have to be involved with financial arrangements at the wedding amid all the excitement. See if you can arrange for overtime to be billed and paid for by check later on.

Go over all contingencies carefully, such as time minimums (two hours is standard) and overtime charges per musician. Two hours may sound like a long time for the pre-reception and ceremonial music alone, but you'd be amazed at how quickly time flies from the arrival of the first guest to the conclusion of the ceremony and recessional. For the reception itself, plan on at least three to four hours.

KEY QUESTIONS FOR BANDS

1. **"What styles of music do you generally play?"**

    If you're looking for jazz and pop, make sure the group can accommodate this. If you decide to hire musicians to play ethnic music for the ceremony or prelude, you may have to hire someone else for the dance numbers for your reception. Lots of musicians might tell you that they play all styles, but don't just take their word for it. Make sure you actually hear them play the styles you want.

2. **"How many band members do you recommend for my wedding?"**

   Describe the room and the size and setting of your wedding exactly to the bandleader or person you're interviewing. There's no sense in hiring a band too big for the room. On the other hand, if you want a big sound in a big room, make that clear in your discussion. Remember, though, that everyone's coming to see *you* on your wedding day, not the band. The band may make the party, but not if you make the band the star!

3. **"How long have the musicians been playing together?"**

   The longer musicians have actually played together, the better they'll sound. Adding even one new player changes the dynamic of the group and some bands will need time to readjust, especially if the new musician is unfamiliar with the repertoire.

4. **"Will you learn new material and, if so, will you rehearse it before the wedding?"**

   What is their attitude about learning new material from sheet music or a tape you provide if you have favorite songs or selections they're not familiar with? The important part of this question is not whether they'll agree to play new material, but whether they'll take the time and trouble to learn and rehearse the new material together before the wedding. It would not be out of line for them to charge for lead sheets (sheet music) if all you can supply is a tape of the song, but it's best to get their commitment to the quality of their performance. Therefore, ask if they'll give you a written guarantee that they will rehearse your special songs before the wedding. The last thing you want is to have the musicians fumbling their way through your special song.

5. **"What is your definition of *continuous* music?"**

Some bands will only play forty-five minutes out of each hour. Others will play longer, but in all cases, arrange for one of the musicians to play during breaks. Playing CDs during breaks can be just as effective, but check out the selection or supply your own. Get the band's reassurance in writing that there will be no periods of silence (except during the ceremony).

6. **"Who is responsible for the musicians' food, and where will they eat?"**

Usually, you will be required to provide food for the band. This may range from sandwiches to a hot plate depending on your budget and what's convenient or available. If the dinner for your guests is expensive, you don't have to provide the same meal for the musicians. Check with your location staff and caterers for an appropriate menu and suitable dining room for the band. Have the musicians served separately. They shouldn't stand in your buffet line or be served as guests. Make that clear when discussing these issues with the band's representative (and the caterer, if necessary).

KEY QUESTIONS FOR BANDS AND DJS

The following questions are important and appropriate for interviewing both bands and DJs:

1. **"Do you specialize in weddings?"**

If the band or DJ does only an occasional wedding, and more bar mitzvahs, clubs, artists' showcases, or corporate events, they may not have the experience or polish needed for a smooth-flowing wedding program. Stick with professionals who really specialize in weddings, not those who do them only occasionally. In addition to extensive wedding experience, make sure the DJ you hire is not a club DJ but a mobile DJ, one whose expertise and equipment is geared for different locations.

2. **"How long have you been in the wedding music business?"**

    Since you'll be booking a band or DJ a long time in advance, you want to be sure that they will still be in business on your wedding date. Many bands and DJs start up, but not all survive. Look for longevity and references.

3. **"May I contact the couples from the last three weddings you performed?"**

    If this request is refused, be concerned. If their clients had been satisfied, they would probably be happy to comply. If you do get references, be sure to follow through and contact them.

4. **"Do you have audio- and videotape samples of your actual performances?"**

    Listening to and viewing the band or DJ is your first step. If their tapes don't move you, move on. However, even if you like what you hear and see, it's best to hear a band or DJ live, in person. Don't just rely on a tape or CD. This is even more important with a band, for very often, studio equipment can make a tape sound wonderful; only by sitting in on an actual performance can you tell how good (or mediocre) a band really is. An exception may be videotapes of actual wedding footage, which are not usually sound enhanced. Generally, with a DJ, his or her personality will shine through on the videotape. Still, it's always worthwhile to see the band or DJ live to get a sense of their interaction with guests at weddings and their performance vibe. Then, if you like their tapes, ask:

5. **"Where and when can I see you in a live performance?"**

    When auditioning the band or DJ, notice their reactions and how they interact with the audience. Look for openness and enthusiasm. Make sure they take requests wherever possible. Flexibility is very important. When you're discussing important details of your program, are you on the same wavelength? If they're cooperative and make great suggestions and show you even better alternatives, that's positive. If they're resistant, again . . . move on. It's important to have generous, good-natured people around on this day of all days.

6. **"Will I get the same musicians or DJ I saw and heard?"**
Some bands or DJ services have several different groups and you might have heard only one. You don't want to be disappointed by the one who shows up for you, so list the names of the band members, DJ, vocalists, and acceptable substitutes in case of emergency. Make sure that the musicians or DJ you heard are the same you actually hire.

7. **"Do you have a list of the songs in your repertoire from which we can choose?"**
Of course, you should expect to have your favorite selections played. It's a good idea, however, to give them the opportunity and freedom to play some of their repertoire as well, especially during unstructured time when dinner is being served. For this reason, it's important to know what material they know well or have on CD. This will help you judge whether you'll be pleased with their repertoire and give you additional song ideas that you may not have thought of before.

8. **"How long before the wedding starts will you arrive and how late will you stay?"**
Musicians and DJs should be set up and playing music well before the first guest arrives to set the tone and to make the early arriving guests feel welcome and comfortable. Make sure the band/DJ is more than willing to arrive early and stay later (though, of course, they have a right to charge for their time accordingly).

9. **"What will the musicians or DJ wear?"**

   Make it clear that you want the musicians and/or DJ to dress appropriately—whether you are having a formal or an informal wedding. Nikes are not cool, even with a tuxedo. Despite the informality of backyard weddings, jackets should be worn throughout (barring oppressive weather conditions). Tell the bandleader or DJ representative what type of wedding you're having and make sure he or she promises to dress accordingly.

10. **"What equipment will you supply, and what equipment will you need, if any? Will you check out the site if you haven't played there before?"**

    Make sure that the band or DJ will supply and be responsible for all the equipment needed, including speakers and sound systems, rental pianos, instruments, extension cords, and so on. Spell it all out in writing, including everything you are to supply as well. The band or the site where the wedding is to take place may provide the sound system. In either case, make sure you know who is responsible for setting it up and who is responsible for ensuring it's in good working order. Should anything go wrong with the sound at the last minute, you want the one who is in charge and responsible to be there. Make sure the bandleader/DJ will coordinate this for you as part of his or her responsibilities. It's not too much to expect that a good bandleader or DJ will have checked out a site before the date of the wedding if he or she has not previously performed there. Any true professional would consider this a necessary part of his or her duty to be prepared.

11. **"Is the bandleader or DJ an experienced and effective emcee?"**

An important function many bands and DJs will perform is to provide an emcee, or a master of ceremonies. If you are hiring a band or DJ, make sure that they will provide an experienced emcee whose personality and style you like. Don't take anything for granted—preview a tape.

HAVING IT ALL WITH A DJ

If you are looking for great professional sound, maximum versatility, and a more modest price, you'll understand the growing popularity of DJs. DJs come equipped with extensive CD collections, which can be supplemented with your own favorites and new "traditionals" you discover in your planning. You can have it all with a DJ—from the Backstreet Boys to the London Philharmonic. All recorded music in every style is at your disposal.

One of the biggest misconceptions is that DJs are too loud—not so at all. The experienced DJ knows how to please a crowd. The volume control is always within reach, and he or she is at all times aware of guests' reactions and responses to the music and will respond accordingly. In addition, you are certainly free to ask for the level of sound you are comfortable with.

A band's repertoire can't really be compared in its range to a DJ's CD collection, nor is it meant to be. You may want the grandeur of the original sound of a great film score for your cocktail hour or processional, or as background music during dinner. You may also want to hear your favorite artists and recordings. This is where a DJ and great CDs can be most effective. Just make sure, as with any musician or band, that he or she knows and will fulfill your selection requirements.

WHAT DOES A DJ COST?

As with live bands, the range of fees for DJs varies from city to city and will depend on the DJ's own popularity and competence. Generally, the range for four hours in larger cities could be anywhere from $1,000 to $1,500 and up for the trendier performance DJs. There may be some up-and-coming DJs who are wonderfully effective but have not yet developed a reputation who may be available for a little less than the going rate in your location. In smaller cities, the minimum might be as low as $595 for four hours. Figure at least $125 an hour and a minimum of two to three hours.

Kemp Harshman of the ADJA (American DJ Association, 888-922-ADJA) advises wariness of unknown companies who promise you the moon for $200 to $300 for four hours. Very often they send out inexperienced beginners who play low-quality, illegally copied tapes and CDs. The RIAA (Recording Industry Artists Association) is clamping down on this and rightly so, for this is a violation of copyright law. Make sure that you meet with the DJ you are actually hiring and see a live performance or at least a videotape of his or her work at a wedding.

With DJs (and bands), you get what you pay for. The last thing you want is what is known in the trade as a "weekend warrior"—the amateurish DJ moonlighting on the weekends who promises four to six hours for $300. In most cases, he or she will not have what it takes or the professional polish to be an effective emcee or DJ.

A good DJ will have great equipment in addition to extra-large speakers and an extensive collection of CDs. Some have spectacular lighting and can offer an array of effects, video backgrounds, and even additional dancers and entertainers. (For a list of the minimum equipment every DJ should have, see question number one on page 54).

NEWER DJ TRENDS

As described in *Rhythm and News,* the newsletter published by Hank Lane Music and Production in New York City, one of the foremost celebrity and society music services, there has been a new trend in recent years to create a hybrid form of music entertainment for weddings and other affairs—the mixture of DJs and live music. This is not alternating a live band with a DJ, but a DJ integrating one or two live musicians and vocalists who perform to prerecorded music. By using polished, ultraprofessional music tracks or backgrounds (like karaoke) and adding the excitement of live performers, a DJ can provide the best of both worlds: a spectacular show with the variety and versatility of a CD collection, and the energy and magic of live entertainers.

KEY QUESTIONS FOR DJS

I. **"What special equipment do you provide?"**

    When interviewing DJs, it's a good idea to refer to this list of equipment. They should provide (at a minimum):

    > Dual CD players (two)
    >
    > Amplifier
    >
    > Two speakers (large enough for the room)
    >
    > Corded microphone
    >
    > Cordless microphone
    >
    > Cordless headset/microphone
    >
    > Mixing board (to adjust and fine-tune sound quality)
    >
    > Back-up gear

2. **"What repertoire of CDs do you offer?"**

Make sure that the DJ's collection of CDs is one that appeals to you and is varied enough to take into account the different tastes of your guests. If it seems dated, or just not for you, find a DJ more compatible with your taste in music. Look at the list of songs he or she suggests for different highlights of the wedding and during dinner and dance sequences. If there is more than enough to choose from, you like the collection, and you sense that you and the DJ see eye to eye, those are good signs. If you're not sure, keep looking.

3. **"If you act as the emcee, will you have a back-up or an assistant to help you?"**

Though DJs are adept at juggling the job of lining up records and following the program, if the DJ is acting as emcee, it's important that there be an assistant to help. The better DJs will have a back-up when they take on the commitment of directing a larger crowd.

BAND-DJ COMBINATION

Another trend is to have a band and DJ alternate and work the program cooperatively, splitting every hour either thirty minutes each (30/30) or forty minutes for one and twenty minutes for the other (40/20). The band and DJ may both be part of the same organization or music service, or be hired independently of each other. If you hire a DJ to work with your band, or vice versa, make sure that both are willing and experienced at working in cooperative situations. Don't hire anyone who demonstrates any resistance or attitude about working with someone else. Your wedding is more important than his or her ego!

The band-DJ combination offers true continuous music (not just fill-ins on breaks) as well as a great change of pace. You can have both the original sound of your favorite dance records, oldies, and top hits that the DJ offers, and the smooth magical sound of a live band and singer performing beautiful ballads.

Having the best of both worlds with the band-DJ combination has become quite popular in the Northeast, though it is available all over the country.

The DJ's extensive knowledge of the latest in recorded music and of the classics of jazz, pop, show tunes, instrumentals, film soundtracks, golden oldies, swing, and ethnic music of all denominations is unsurpassed. A band musician is dedicated to playing live music incomparably well, and DJs are dedicated to acquiring knowledge of the world of recorded music. Both are trained at knowing what will best please you and your guests. The combination of the two is unbeatable.

REVIEW—QUESTIONS FOR BANDS

1. What styles of music do you generally play?
2. How many band members do you recommend for my wedding?
3. How long have the musicians been playing together?
4. Will you learn new material and, if so, will you rehearse it before the wedding?
5. What is your definition of *continuous* music?
6. Who is responsible for the musicians' food, and where will they eat?

REVIEW—QUESTIONS FOR BANDS AND DJS

1. Do you specialize in weddings?
2. How long have you been in the wedding music business?
3. May I contact the couples from the last three weddings you performed?
4. Do you have audio- and videotape samples of your actual performances?
5. Where and when can I see you in a live performance?
6. Will I get the same musicians or DJ I saw and heard?

7. Do you have a list of the songs in your repertoire from which we can choose?

8. How long before the wedding starts will you arrive and how late will you stay?

9. What will the musicians or DJ wear?

10. What equipment will you supply, and what equipment will you need, if any? Will you check out the site if you haven't played there before?

11. Is the bandleader or DJ an experienced and effective emcee?

REVIEW—QUESTIONS FOR DJS

1. What special equipment do you provide?

2. What repertoire of CDs do you offer?

3. If you act as the emcee, will you have a back-up or an assistant to help you?

THE MASTER OF CEREMONIES—"EMCEE"

Regardless of whether you have live music, a DJ, or a combination of both, an emcee or someone guiding the events is an absolute necessity to make your wedding flow smoothly and to highlight special moments and events at the reception. An emcee does more than merely make announcements: It takes a special talent, personality, and sense of timing to inspire a large group of people of all ages, musical tastes, and backgrounds to participate. Guests easily become bored when an emcee fails to command their full attention during the highlights of the wedding.

If you're not hiring a band or DJ and intend to have a friend or relative play CDs at the wedding, consider hiring a professional emcee. There are professional speaker services listed in most area yellow pages. Through these organizations, you can get direct information about hiring emcees in your area.

Planning Tip

If your DJ doesn't show up (unfortunately, it's been known to happen), you can call the Emergency Disc Jockey Hot Line in Southern California (and increasingly in other areas) at 800-949-3249. They promise to return your call within ten minutes and provide music within ninety minutes. For information and availability in your area, contact your local chapter of the American Disc Jockey Association (ADJA).

Think twice before you have a friend or relative act as emcee. It's a real commitment if done properly, and your friend may not have the experience or know-how to encourage full participation in the reception events, he or she might even develop stage fright.

Many DJs and bandleaders are talented singers and entertainers in their own right and have the ability to be great emcees as well. It's also important to interview the emcee and to see him or her at a wedding to make sure his or her personality suits you. Some emcees may not be as dignified as you'd like. On the other hand, some may be too low-key for your taste.

One great reason to find the best DJ or band you can afford is that you can rely on the better ones to provide the emcee for you. This will also give you one less person (and one less contract) to deal with. If budget considerations are a strong factor, save money on the *number* of musicians and people you hire, not on their quality. A DJ or bandleader who is a great emcee can make your wedding a great success.

CONTRACTS: GET WHAT YOU BARGAIN FOR IN WRITING

The points listed below should be spelled out in the contract. When signing any contract, you can't rely on such verbal representations or assurances as "Don't worry—this clause doesn't mean anything." In almost all states, if not every state, what's in writing is legally what you have agreed to when you sign. That also means that if you're told "We'll include that—no need to put it in writing," make sure you put it in writing anyway. If it's not actually written into the contract, you won't have a leg to stand on if they don't follow through on their verbal commitment.

As with all contracts, read the fine print carefully and make sure you understand everything. If there's something you're unsure of, don't sign until you're very clear on what it means and that it's exactly what you have agreed to beforehand. If a representative or the bandleader explains something to you orally, and the wording of the contract is contradictory or confusing, have him or her rewrite that clause so that it clearly conforms to your original agreement.

Feel free to ask lots of questions. Insist on having any confusing word, sentence, or paragraph changed or deleted until the contract is clear and accurate. Too many contracts are not well written or have clauses no one should agree to. (See Wedding Insurance, page 60.) Don't sign anything until you are comfortable with every word of the document. (You can also refer to the sample contract in Appendix B.)

MUSIC CONTRACT CHECKLIST

1. Specify the day, time, and location.

2. Note the exact start time (include setting up) and when overtime would kick in.

3. State the rate per hour and overtime costs per hour (per person or per entire band/DJ service).

4. List actual name of the DJ and/or every member of the band and/or instrument(s) they are to bring and play; list the substitutes acceptable in case of emergency.

5. List all equipment they are to bring and be responsible for, and detail what you have agreed to provide.

6. Describe the emcee/coordinator's duties; include your requirement for a planning session to write out your wedding program and for a printout of the program (and script).

7. State explicitly when and for which parts of the ceremony and/or reception the band/DJ will be performing (after ceremony for cocktails, before or during dinner, and so on).

8. List the number and duration of breaks and whether live or taped music will be played; get an agreement in writing that there will be no periods of silence. DJs do not take musical breaks; they provide prerecorded segments when short breaks are necessary.

9. Name the special songs they have promised to play and agreed to rehearse.

10. Specify the dress requirements.

11. Carefully review cancellation and refund policy.

12. Specify that you are not liable for personal damage or damage to equipment by third parties, such as the caterer, the guests, the parking attendant, the hotel staff, and so on.

WEDDING INSURANCE

Some contracts contain clauses that would make you financially responsible for *any and all* damage to the musicians' or DJ's equipment caused by *anyone* during the wedding. This would put you in a financially vulnerable position if anything unforeseen were to happen. More and more catering establishments and hotels are insisting that the bride and groom take out a policy naming them (the caterer, and so on) as the coinsured to protect them from any liability as well.

You can try to make sure the musicians and DJs are insured and that you are not liable for anything except, of course, your own negligent behavior or, at most, a small deductible as provided for in their insurance policy. Have them show you a certificate of insurance. However, that still may not satisfy the hotel or caterer.

The best alternative is a wedding insurance policy. It not only covers you for liability and property damage, it also protects you from financial responsibility in case of cancellation by reimbursing your deposits, and so on. This type of policy is underwritten by the Firemen's Fund. For further information and accurate details, call: 800-ENGAGED (800-364-2433).

WEDDING MUSIC PLANNING CALENDAR

FOR LARGE EVENTS AND BUSY SEASONS

One year to eighteen months before the wedding—or as soon as possible:

1. Start preliminary music program planning.
2. Look for and book your location.
3. Look for and book the band or DJ of your choice. (Two weeks later: Make sure confirmation and/or contract is received.)

FOR SMALLER EVENTS AND SLOWER TIMES OF YEAR

Nine months before the wedding—or as soon as possible:

Steps 1, 2, and 3 as outlined above.

FOR ALL WEDDINGS

Four to six weeks before the event:

1. Meet with your band or DJ and emcee and work out your final program and script with all announcements, word for word.

2. Get written copies of fully detailed program and announcements (script).

3. Reconfirm equipment details and the date fee balances are due.

4. Arrange rehearsal dates for special performances (if applicable).

5. Make sure the band or DJ has all CDs, tapes, and sheet music required for your final program and for rehearsing your special material.

Notes and Reminders

_____

_____

_____

_____

_____

_____

_____

_____

_____

_____

_____

_____

_____

_____

_____

_____

_____

_____

_____

The music of love is heard in the rhythm of a heartbeat . . . in the melody of a sigh.

Chapter Four

WORKBOOK I: THE DREAM— YOUR PRELIMINARY PROGRAM

*N*ow that you've learned the most important fundamentals, it's time to turn to Workbook I. The workbooks were designed to simplify the process of successful wedding music planning. They will help you create a magical musical program for the wedding of your dreams, systematically and easily. Your first step is to make a wish list—your preliminary plan. Have fun with it and let your imagination be your guide.

IT'S NOT HOW MUCH YOU SPEND . . . IT'S HOW CREATIVELY YOU SPEND

While financial considerations are an obvious factor in making most wedding decisions for all but the wealthiest of families, your wedding can and will be a marvelous emotional musical experience even if you have a tightly limited budget. For example, if you're planning to be married in a church or synagogue, there may be an organist or choir, fully experienced in wedding programs, available for a modest fee or donation. In addition, it's amazing how friends, and friends of friends, appear with all sorts of talent at your disposal. You may want to consider asking one to perform or even host as an emcee or DJ. (As we pointed out earlier, have a friend act as emcee only if he or she is experienced and you know for certain he or she won't freeze or fall apart in the spotlight.) But don't even think of emceeing your own wedding!

You may find in your own CD collection a treasure trove of fine music perfect for all parts of your wedding, from the ceremony to the last dance. Today, with the availability of sophisticated electronic equipment at reasonable prices, you can rent or buy a CD player (and complete sound system) very reasonably and program well over five hours of continuous music. There are literally thousands of selections to choose from, perfect for dinner and dance receptions, which can make your wedding as exciting and wonderful as you have ever dreamed it would be, even on the tightest of budgets.

You can have a soloist play during the prelude of your wedding and have a DJ/emcee play wonderful dance music, romantic love songs, and film soundtracks even for a large reception and still keep your music budget around $1,000 or less.

What to Do Next: Step-by-Step — Follow the Yellow Brick Road

1. Discuss your ideas with your fiancé and anyone else you'd like to involve in your planning (family, friends, or professional coordinators). Remember one thing, however: It's your wedding. Don't listen to anyone without checking honestly with each other and searching your own hearts for the answers you need.

2. Fill out the worksheets in Workbook I. They're broken down into sections for each part of the wedding. You may or may not want a prelude or an interlude. You may be undecided at this stage. That's fine. There's plenty of time for maybes.

3. Make some tentative song selections by referring to the list of favorite songs you've started and by looking at the song lists in Appendix A.

When you have finished filling out your preliminary program (your wish list), you'll be ready to shop for and interview musicians, bands, and DJs. Your guide will have all the information you need, so remember to take it along with you for interviews and meetings. If you haven't found a location yet, keep looking and find one as soon as possible.

Workbook I: A Wish List

YOUR WEDDING—FROM PRELUDE TO RECEPTION

Prelude

Yes ☐   No ☐   Maybe ☐

Time of Day/How Long _____

Ideal Setting _____

_____

_____

Food/Cocktails/Refreshments _____

_____

_____

Style and Mood We Would Like to Create _____

_____

_____

_____

_____

Possible Song Selections _____

_____

_____

_____

_____

Favorite Instruments/CDs _____

_____

_____

_____

Notes/Ideas/Questions _____

_____

_____

_____

_____

Pre-processional

Time of Day/How Long _____

Ideal Setting_____

_____

_____

Clergy/Special People/Family and Friends _____

_____

_____

_____

Possible Song Selections _____

_____

_____

_____

Favorite Instruments/CDs _____

_____

_____

_____

_____

Notes/Ideas/Questions _____

_____

_____

_____

_____

_____

_____

Processional

Time of Day/How Long _____

Ideal Setting_____

_____

_____

Wedding Party

Family _____

_____

_____

_____

Maid of Honor _____   Flower Girl _____

Bridesmaids

_____   _____

_____   _____

_____   _____

_____   _____

_____   _____

Best Man_____   Ring Bearer _____

Groomsmen/Ushers

_____   _____
_____   _____
_____   _____
_____   _____
_____   _____

Style and Mood We Would Like to Create _____
_____
_____
_____

Possible Song Selections _____
_____
_____

Favorite Instruments/CDs _____
_____
_____

Notes/Ideas/Questions _____
_____
_____

Ceremony

Time of Day/How Long _____

Ideal Setting _____

_____

_____

Special Performances/Prayers/Songs   When and Who Performs

_____   _____

_____   _____

_____   _____

Notes/Ideas/Questions _____

_____

_____

Unity Candle

Yes ☐   No ☐   Maybe ☐

Possible Song Selections _____

_____

_____

Favorite Instruments/CDs _____

_____

_____

Notes/Ideas/Questions _____

_____

_____

Recessional

Possible Song Selections _____

_____

_____

_____

CDs _____

_____

_____

_____

Instrument Change from Processional (if any) _____

_____

_____

_____

Notes/Ideas/Questions _____

_____

_____

_____

_____

_____

_____

_____

_____

_____

_____

Interlude

Yes ☐   No ☐   Maybe ☐   Receiving Line   Yes ☐   No ☐   Maybe ☐

Cocktail Reception   Yes ☐   No ☐   Maybe ☐

Time of Day/How Long _____

Ideal Setting_____

_____

_____

Style and Mood We Would Like to Create _____

_____

_____

_____

_____

_____

Favorite Instruments/CDs _____

_____

_____

_____

_____

_____

_____

Possible Song Selections _____

_____

_____

_____

_____

_____

_____

_____

Notes/Ideas/Questions _____

_____

_____

_____

_____

_____

_____

_____

_____

_____

Reception

Time of Day/How Long _____

Ideal Setting _____

_____

_____

Style and Mood We Would Like to Create _____

_____

_____

_____

Formal Dinner _____

_____

_____

Buffet Dinner _____

_____

_____

Other _____

_____

_____

Our Arrival/Introduction

Possible Song Selections _____

_____

_____

_____

Our First Dance

Possible Song Selections _____

_____

_____

_____

Family Dances (Wedding Party)

Possible Song Selections _____

_____

_____

_____

Ethnic Dance Numbers

Possible Song Selections _____

_____

_____

_____

Dinner Music

Possible Song Selections _____

_____

_____

_____

Ballroom Dances

Favorite Dances _____

_____

_____

_____

Possible Song Selections _____

_____

_____

_____

_____

_____

Group Dances

Possible Song Selections _____

_____

_____

_____

_____

_____

Other Dances

Possible Song Selections _____

_____

_____

_____

_____

_____

Other Possible Song Selections _____

_____

_____

Family Candle-Lighting Ceremony_____

_____

_____

Special Song Tribute _____

_____

Cutting the Cake _____

_____

_____

Tossing the Bouquet   Garter Toss

_____   _____

_____   _____

The Last Dance _____

_____

_____

_____

Circle of Love Ceremony _____

_____

_____

_____

_____

_____

Notes/Ideas/Questions _____

_____

_____

_____

_____

_____

_____

_____

_____

_____

_____

_____

_____

_____

_____

Notes and Reminders

_____

_____

_____

_____

_____

_____

_____

_____

_____

_____

_____

_____

_____

_____

_____

_____

_____

_____

_____

_____

Love is borne on the music of the night.

—Anonymous

Chapter Five

$\mathcal{W}$ORKBOOK II:
THE DREAM COMES INTO VIEW

$\mathcal{N}$ow that you've read chapters 1 through 3 and have filled out the worksheets in Workbook I (your wish list), you probably have an idea of the kind of wedding you would like. You're ready to call and interview bands and DJs. Your guide will have everything you need for making this next part of the process easy and simple. You should have:

1. A wish list (your preliminary program)

2. Ideas for song selections

3. Key questions for bands and/or DJs

4. A contract checklist (to be used when interviewing bands and/or DJs)

5. A checklist and notes and reminders about the location you have booked or are considering

HOW TO USE WORKBOOK II

Workbook II was designed to be filled out when you interview musicians, bands, and/or DJs. The purpose of this workbook is simply for you to keep all your important information organized and handy. We've broken the worksheets down into pages for each part of the wedding—the prelude, ceremony, interlude, and reception. This will accommodate as many possibilities as you need to explore. Everyone's experience is different. You may find what you're looking for after your first call to a friend whose wedding musicians you decide to use. Or you may interview as many as two or three DJs, a soloist, and a band as well. There are no hard-and-fast rules. Just write down and keep track of as much information as you can when you are making calls and interviewing or auditioning musicians and DJs. You will save yourself the most time and energy by keeping track of everything and using the workbooks in order.

Even if you think you know that you'll be using a particular band or DJ (or simply having a friend help you), it's still a good idea to take your wish list out there to check prices and to see what else is available. Interview some bands and DJs and weigh the advantages and disadvantages of each, as well as the band-DJ combination. It's a great way to generate creative ideas of your own and to build even more confidence in organizing your wedding music program.

Interviewing and auditioning experienced musicians and DJs will help you decide between live music, a DJ, or a combination of both. A good way to meet them is to attend a bridal show in your area. They're fun and you'll walk away with lots of ideas and other contacts as well. Check the resources in Appendix C for bridal show information.

Even if you think you can't afford live music or a DJ, meet with one or two soloists before making your final decisions. Consider all options and you may be pleasantly surprised at what you find available and affordable.

What to Do Next

1. Review the lists of key questions for bands and DJs on pages 56 and 57 and your preliminary program—the wish list you filled out in Workbook I.

2. Start following leads and calling and interviewing bands. (The guide was meant to be taken with you—it's extremely portable with plenty of room for note taking.)

3. Every time you interview or audition a band or DJ, fill out a column on a DJ or band possibilities worksheet (pages 90 to 101), writing down names and important information. Fill out as many of the band and DJ options columns as you need. Write down any band/DJ music recommendations you particularly like on pages 102 and 103.

4. After your interviews and auditions, when you've gathered enough information to start making some music decisions:
   a. Narrow down your song choices.
   b. Go on to chapter 6 for key points in deciding on the band or DJ for you.

WORKSHEETS

CEREMONY POSSIBILITIES—CHURCH OR TEMPLE			
Church / Temple	*#1*	*#2*	*#3*
Name Address Phone			
Music Director/ Coordinator Interview Date			
Special Requests Fees Musician/ Instrument Fees			

CEREMONY POSSIBILITIES—CHURCH OR TEMPLE

Church / Temple	#1	#2	#3
Soloist Fees			
Choir Fees			
Outside Musician Fees			
Rehearsal Time Fees			
Cancellation Policy			
Date Deposit Is Due			
Date Balance Is Due			

PRELUDE AND CEREMONY—BAND/MUSICIAN POSSIBILITIES

	Band option #1	Band option #2	Band option #3
Name Address			
Phone Contact			
Interview Date			
Our First Impression			
Attitude—Rapport			
Instrument(s)—Style			
Names of Performers and Musicians We Auditioned			

PRELUDE AND CEREMONY—BAND/MUSICIAN POSSIBILITIES

	Band option #1	Band option #2	Band option #3
Special Requests Charges			
Equipment Needed Equipment Supplied			
Number of Hours			
Musicians' Attire			
Cancellation Policy			
Cartage Fees			
Total Fees			
Date Deposit Is Due			
Date Balance Is Due			

PRELUDE AND CEREMONY—DJ POSSIBILITIES

	DJ option #1	DJ option #2	DJ option #3
Name Address			
Phone Contact			
Interview Date			
Our First Impression			
Attitude—Rapport			
Impression of Style and CD Collection			
Special Requests Charges			

PRELUDE AND CEREMONY—DJ POSSIBILITIES

	DJ option #1	DJ option #2	DJ option #3
Equipment Needed Equipment Supplied			
Number of Hours			
DJ's Attire			
Cancellation Policy			
Cartage Fees			
Total Fees			
Date Deposit Is Due			
Date Balance Is Due			

INTERLUDE—BAND/MUSICIAN POSSIBILITIES

	Band option #1	*Band option #2*	*Band option #3*
Name Address			
Phone Contact			
Interview Date			
Our First Impression			
Attitude—Rapport			
Instrument(s)—Style			
Names of Performers and Musicians We Auditioned			

INTERLUDE—BAND/MUSICIAN POSSIBILITIES

	Band option #1	*Band option #2*	*Band option #3*
Special Requests Charges			
Equipment Needed Equipment Supplied			
Number of Hours			
Musicians' Attire			
Cancellation Policy			
Cartage Fees			
Total Fees			
Date Deposit Is Due			
Date Balance Is Due			

INTERLUDE—DJ POSSIBILITIES

	DJ option #1	DJ option #2	DJ option #3
Name Address			
Phone Contact			
Interview Date			
Our First Impression			
Attitude—Rapport			
Impression of Style and CD Collection			
Special Requests Charges			

INTERLUDE—DJ POSSIBILITIES

	DJ option #1	DJ option #2	DJ option #3
Equipment Needed Equipment Supplied			
Number of Hours			
DJ's Attire			
Cancellation Policy			
Cartage Fees			
Total Fees			
Date Deposit Is Due			
Date Balance Is Due			

RECEPTION—BAND/MUSICIAN POSSIBILITIES

	Band option #1	*Band option #2*	*Band option #3*
Name Address			
Phone Contact			
Interview Date Our First Impression			
Attitude—Rapport			
Instruments—Style			
Number of Musicians			
Names of Musicians We Auditioned			

RECEPTION—BAND/MUSICIAN POSSIBILITIES

	Band option #1	Band option #2	Band option #3
Number of Hours			
Length of Sets			
Number of Sets			
Charges for Special Requests			
Continuous Music Extra Charges			
Equipment Needed Equipment Supplied			
Cartage Fees			
Musicians' Attire			
Cancellation Policy			
Overtime per Musician			
Overtime per Hour Total			
Date Deposit Is Due			
Date Balance Is Due			

RECEPTION—DJ POSSIBILITIES

	DJ option #1	*DJ option #2*	*DJ option #3*
Name Address			
Phone Contact			
Interview Date Our First Impression			
Attitude—Rapport			
Impression of Style and CD Collection			
Special Requests Charges			

RECEPTION—DJ POSSIBILITIES

	DJ option #1	DJ option #2	DJ option #3
Number of Performers (Vocalists/Dancers and/or Musicians)			
Number of Hours			
Equipment Needed Equipment Supplied Extra Lighting Fees Other Extras			
Cartage Fees			
DJ's Attire			
Cancellation Policy			
Overtime per Hour Total			
Date Deposit Is Due			
Date Balance Is Due			

Band/DJ Music Recommendations

Prelude

_____

_____

_____

_____

_____

_____

_____

_____

Ceremony

_____

_____

_____

_____

_____

_____

_____

Band/DJ Music Recommendations

Interlude

_____

_____

_____

_____

_____

_____

_____

_____

Reception

_____

_____

_____

_____

_____

_____

_____

_____

NARROWING DOWN OUR MUSIC CHOICES			
	#1	*#2*	*#3*
Prelude			
Pre-Processional			
Ceremony (Solo)			
Unity Candle			
Recessional			
Interlude			
Reception			
Our Arrival/Introduction			
Our First Dance			
Our Parents' Dance			
Must Play			
Group Dances			
Must Have			

NARROWING DOWN OUR MUSIC CHOICES

	#1	#2	#3
Ethnic Dances			
Other Special Dances			
Other Special Moments and/or Toasts			
Cake Cutting			
Bouquet Toss			
Garter Toss			
Last Dance			
Other			

Notes and Reminders

Notes and Reminders

Dreams were for fools—they could never come true, until I was loved by you.

—"Until I Was Loved by You," 1997 Emmy Award—winning song of the year, by Gloria Sklerov and Stan Bush

Chapter Six

WORKBOOK III:
MAKING THE DREAM A REALITY

MAKING FINAL CHOICES —
MUSICIANS, BAND, AND/OR DJ

*N*ow that you have filled out Workbook II, you have narrowed down your choices for the emcee, band/musicians, and/or DJ. Now the question is, "How do we decide?"

One way to decide on a musician is to think of the mood and atmosphere you want to create and choose one or more instruments that most appeal to you. Then consider the repertoire, the experience of the musician or soloist, the source of the referral, and his or her references. If you like what you heard during the audition, if his or her answers to your questions were appropriate, and you feel a natural rapport, chances are your choice will become obvious to you.

A good rule of thumb for the reception comes from independent DJ Mike Carcano of Carcano Entertainment in Southern California. His advice is to carefully consider the personality of the emcee, DJ, or bandleader you hire. You must click with him or her. When you view a tape of a performance at a wedding, does it have the tone you would feel comfortable with? Is there too much talking and joking for your taste? Is the DJ/emcee more subdued and refined? Too dull, too low-key, or boring? Does the emcee have the guests "in the palm of his or her hand"? Mike believes that the most important characteristic of a great DJ is the ability to read the room, especially in today's multicultural society. The DJ is not there just to play music or make a few announcements. Each group needs a different approach. DJs and emcees can make or break a party. View as many tapes as you can of each person you interview. Pretty soon, you will know.

Naturally, at this stage of the planning, you'll have a better idea about what everything else is going to cost and a pretty good idea of how much your music budget is. In light of that, there are many options that are best discussed with your family and fiancé. Perhaps your family is paying for the wedding and you want to be conservative in handling costs, concerned that this may put too much of a strain on their budget or your own. Whatever you decide, you've done your homework and you know now that no matter how little you have to spend on music, your program is going to be wonderful.

Read chapter 1 again and imagine the "scenes" of your wedding now that you have more information. Before deciding, review the list of instrumental combinations in chapter 2.

Making Final Choices — Song and Music Selections

Choosing the selections for your wedding is a natural creative process that will unfold as you develop a sense of what's right for you. First, sort through and evaluate the music and song recommendations from your own lists and from the musicians and DJs you've interviewed.

You have plenty of time to enjoy listening to music and imagining lots of possibilities until your final planning meeting with your musicians/DJ (two to six weeks before the wedding, depending on how many special requests you have and new songs they must learn). If you're torn between two selections for one of the special moments you're planning, such as your first dance or the processional, consider using both. There's no rule that you must play only one selection as you walk down the aisle, or one song for your first dance. And don't worry . . . you have lots of time. These decisions don't have to be made until the final planning session. You can feel confident in whatever decisions you make, knowing you've combined the best of both worlds: listening to your heart *and* the professionals. Always remember that you can play whatever music you love even if it isn't your bandleader's choice.

What to Do Next

1. Book the band of your choice as soon as possible.
2. Make sure you get a confirmation in the mail within two weeks so you know the band is definitely booked. If not, call to make sure your date is secured.
3. Keep listening to music and narrowing down your choices for each category.

4. Two to six weeks before the wedding, schedule an appointment with the band/DJ and/or emcee for a planning session to firm up your final program. For this meeting, bring:

    a. Your guide with Workbook II filled out.

    b. All your notes and ideas and your list of song choices so far.

    c. Any CDs, tapes, or sheet music to be included in the program or needed by the musicians for rehearsal. (Schedule a rehearsal date and time for any soloists or special performances you have arranged.)

    d. The names of everyone in your wedding party and relatives and friends you want to acknowledge or introduce. Next to each name, spell out the correct pronunciation phonetically.

FINAL CHOICES FOR BAND/DJ/SOLOIST/EMCEE

	Prelude	*Ceremony*	*Interlude*	*Reception*
Name				
Contact				
Address				
Telephone				
Total Cost				

How to Use Workbook III—Writing the Script for Your Final Program

Workbook III, your final program, is meant to be filled out with your bandleader, DJ, and/or emcee at the final planning session around two to six weeks before the wedding. Even if you're planning a small wedding and not hiring a band or DJ, fill out Workbook III with your fiancé and anyone else helping with the music. Write out *word for word* what the emcee is to say and what the musicians are to play. Just as a director leaves nothing to chance and won't start shooting a film without a script, you need to write out the program you envision as well—your "script." Everyone participating should know what to say, what to do, and when to do it.

If you want to acknowledge a relative's birthday, recognize someone who introduced the two of you, or thank friends and relatives who have traveled from afar to be with you, make sure you write that out with your emcee, bandleader, and/or DJ. These warm personal touches mean a lot and will be appreciated. Don't count on verbal instructions to be remembered at the wedding. There'll be too much going on. The extra thirty minutes or so that it takes to write out your program will be the most important thirty minutes in your planning, for they will guarantee the success of your wedding program and make yours a wedding to remember.

Not only should the announcements be written out word for word with phonetic spellings next to each name, the schedule of all the events (special moments and dance segments) should be timed as closely as possible. The object is to allow the band/DJ/emcee enough flexibility to pace the party and to use judgment in reading the room, and at the same time ensure that the pace and energy of the party keeps flowing.

By giving everyone, including the photographer and videographer, a copy of the script, you will ensure that the emcee/bandleader/DJ will coordinate all the important moments and highlights of the reception. Nothing should happen without the emcee announcing it and the photographer/videographer taking pictures of it. Therefore, it's a good idea to advise your photographer/videographer to coordinate with the emcee/bandleader/DJ as well. We cannot stress enough the importance of a script to guarantee the success of your wedding program. Not only is it important for you to insist on a written script, it is also important for you to insist on having the wedding program planned and carried out the way you, your fiancé, and family would prefer. Don't be intimidated by caterers, coordinators, or musicians about things that are important to you.

Many bands and DJs have program forms of their own. However, they may not provide as detailed a script as you would like to follow. Also, theirs may not be tailor-made for your wedding. Regardless of the form you use, the most important elements are to make sure that all your ideas and decisions are incorporated and that your script is written down word for word. We have provided worksheets that are open and flexible enough for you to work out your own order of events and all your special moments.

The sequence of events and style of wedding receptions in your area will vary, as will your own personal tastes; there are no hard-and-fast rules. Every family is different and every couple will

Planning Tip

After planning the music for the highlights and special moments of a four-hour reception, you can usually expect to have two additional hours of music, or approximately twenty-five to thirty songs. Include your "must haves," but give the band or DJ discretion to come up with ideas of his or her own and take requests.

have different preferences. What follows is an actual program and script filled out by the bride and groom with the bandleader/emcee at their final meeting. A professional band or DJ will actually work from this scheduled outline of your wedding program. This sample program will be helpful in giving you an idea of how to judge the length of time and pacing for each part of the wedding.

This particular wedding program worked out beautifully. Guests marveled at what a wonderful time they had for weeks afterward, and the music was complimented as a key part of the wedding's success by literally everyone who attended. You can see how carefully some of the details were considered and yet how flexible the program was during and after dinner.

Sample Wedding Program

Wedding Date: Sept. 17, 2000

Location: Westlake Village Inn

Address:

Time: 3 P.M.

Phone:

Setup Time: 2:45 P.M.

	Song / Music	*Soloist / Musician*
Prelude (Seating of Guests)	Play appropriate classical and semiclassical selections, including: "Greensleeves, Prelude in C" "Air in G, Clair de Lune"	Two musicians: keyboard and flute

Time: 3 P.M. sharp

Location: Garden next to gazebo

When all the guests are seated (approximately 3:20 P.M.):

Play CD "The Wedding Song"

Pre-Processional

Number of Participants: Four

Participants in Order of Entrance: Grandma and Grandpa M., Grandma S. and Uncle Allen

Play CD "Arioso"

	Song / Music	*Soloist / Musician*

Processional

Number of Participants: Fifteen

Participants in Order of Entrance: Rabbi F. and Reverend R.; Grandma and Grandpa M.; Grandma S.; best man, Rick M.; groom's parents and groom, Gloria and Jerry and Keith; groomsmen and bridesmaids (coupled), Ken and Terry, Karen and Kevin; maid of honor, Veronica H.; flower girl, Morgan; bride's parents, Joan and Bob, joined by the bride, Kelli.

	Pachelbel's "Canon in D"	
Until entrance of flower girl, then:	"Minuet in G" (Mozart)	
Play through entrance of bride's parents		

Bride's Entrance

"Bridal Chorus" from *Lohengrin*
("Here Comes the Bride")

Ceremony

Invocation/prayer

Play CD "Coming Home"

Unity Candle—Lighting Ceremony

Play CD "Yours, Mine, and Ours"

To be sung by
Robin T. to instrumental

Recessional

"The Wedding March"
"Irish Washerwoman"

Keyboard/flute
(Musicians)

	Song/Music	*Soloist/Musician*

Interlude (Approximately 3:45–4:45 P.M.)

Location: Patio off main dining room (no receiving line)

	General selections from preselected soft jazz/pop repertoire	Keyboard/saxophone/ guitar

Must-Play Songs: "Through the Eyes of Love"
"Someone to Watch Over Me"

Special instructions: Live music is to continue on the patio until 5 P.M.

DJ plays music (CDs) in the ballroom for the reception from 5–9 P.M.

Reception (DJ takes over for reception.)

Grand Entrance (Approximately 5:15 P.M.)

Participants: Bride and groom

Emcee announces: *Ladies and gentlemen, for the very first time, we take great pleasure in introducing Mr. and Mrs. Kelli and Keith Sklerov.*

"We Are Family" (*Le Cage Aux Folles* CD)

(Everyone applauds as they enter. As the applause subsides start intro for . . .)

First Dance

Participants: Bride and groom only

Play CD "At Last" (Etta James)

As song ends, segue into:

Bridal Party Dance   Play CD "Because You Loved Me"

DJ and emcee instructions: Play the first eight bars of the intro as you call on the bridal party and family to join the bride and groom on the dance floor.

Emcee instructions: Introduce and call to dance floor:

1. Parents of the bride, Joan and Bob M.

2. Parents of the groom, Gloria and Jerry S.

3. Best man and maid of honor, Rick M. and Veronica H.

4. Sister of the groom and husband, Karen and Kevin W.

5. Brother of the bride and wife, Kenny and Terry M.

Emcee instructions: After bridal party dances to first half of "Because You Loved Me":

Emcee announces: *Kelli and Keith invite all their friends and family to join them on the dance floor.*

Emcee instructions: As song ends and everyone is still on the dance floor:

Emcee announces: *Everyone join hands and circle around the bride and groom for the "hora," the traditional Hebrew dance of celebration.*

Emcee instructions: Invite everyone to the dance floor and get circles going around the bride and groom. Encourage everyone to join the bride and groom in the center of the circle. Encourage onlookers to clap.

Play CDs "Hava Nagila," "Hevenu Sholem Aleichem,"

"Simon Tov" (repeat medley as required)

Dance Segment (Approximately 5:45 P.M.)

Foxtrots and medium Latin rhythms as per preselection list:

Must-Play Songs: "I Don't Wanna Miss a Thing" (Aerosmith)

"Just to See Her" (Smokey Robinson)

"Something" (Beatles)

At 6:00 P.M. (or when notified by caterer) emcee announces that dinner is being served and asks everyone to be seated.

Welcoming Toasts (Approximately 6:05 P.M.)

Participants: Bride and groom and both sets of parents

Emcee announces: *We invite Kelli and Keith and both sets of parents to join us on the dance floor.*

Introduce: Kelli and Keith Sklerov

Bob and Joan Murphy

Gloria and Jerry Sklerov

Emcee instructions: When participants are lined up across the dance floor:

Emcee announces: *Kelli and Keith would like to express their gratitude to all their friends and family who have come from great distances to share this special day in their lives. Please stand when your name is called so they can introduce you.*

Emcee instructions: Hand the mike to Kelli or Keith with the list of names.

Note: Check with groom's mother, Gloria. Be sure that everyone sings "Happy Birthday" to Keith's uncle Howard S. before dessert.

Family Toasts

Emcee announces: *The bride and groom and their parents would like to toast each other.*

After toasts:

Emcee announces: *As a special tribute to his bride, the groom has asked a dear family friend, musical theater performer Rhoda Travis, to sing "Love Knows No Wrong" with her son Glenn accompanying her.*

Emcee instructions: During dinner, play appropriate songs from these favorite CDs:

Best of Sade

Dave Koz

Parents' Dance: (Approximately 6:45 P.M. or toward end of dinner)

Emcee announces: *We'd like to invite our bride, Kelli, to dance with her dad, Bob.*

Play CD "My Little Girl"

Emcee instructions: As the song ends . . .

Emcee announces: *And now the groom, Keith, would like to dance with his mom, Gloria.*

Play CD "The Man You've Become"

Emcee instructions: As the song ends . . .

Emcee announces: *We'd like to invite everyone to the dance floor to PARTY!*

Emcee instructions: Throughout reception alternate ballads and up-tempos with group dances from preselected list ("YMCA," "Electric Slide") and singles-only dances when appropriate for pacing. Bride and groom like Steely Dan, Tori Amos, and Alanis Morissette.

Must-Play Songs: "I Only Have Eyes for You"

"Unforgettable"

"You're Still the One"

"Your Love Amazes Me"

Emcee instructions: Lots of variety and crowd participation. Take requests. KEEP ENERGY UP!!!

Anniversary Dance

Participants: Married couples

Emcee instructions: First invite couples married five years to the dance floor; after they dance for a few minutes, invite ten, fifteen, twenty, twenty-five years, until the couple married the longest is invited to dance alone and is congratulated.

Play CD "It Had to Be You"

Cutting the Cake (Approximately 8:00 P.M.)

Play CD "Chapel of Love"

Emcee instructions: As the song plays, invite everyone to gather around Kelli and Keith as they cut the cake.

Bride and Groom Toasts (As cake is served)

Emcee instructions: Call for toasts—Keith and Kelli, best man (Rick M.), and maid of honor (Veronica). Introduce best man and maid of honor for their toasts.

Emcee announces: *Keith would like to make a special toast to his bride, Kelli.*

Bouquet Toss (Approximately 8:30 P.M.)

Participants: Bride and single friends and family

Emcee instructions: Invite females who are single and over the age of eighteen to the dance floor.

Play CD "Isn't She Lovely"

Garter Toss (Approximately 8:40 P.M.)

Participants: Groom and single friends and family

Emcee instructions: Kelli does *not* want a "taking off the garter" ceremony. She will hand the garter to Keith. Handle as you did the bouquet toss.

Play CD "Simply Irresistible" (Robert Palmer)

Last Dance

Participants: Everyone

Emcee instructions: Have everybody link arms in a "circle of love" around the bride and groom for their last dance—wishing them life's blessings. As the music plays, have everyone draw closer and closer around the bride and groom in the circle.

Play CD "Can You Feel the Love Tonight?"

Emcee announces: *Kelli and Keith want to thank everyone for coming and sharing in their special day.* (Hand the mike to Kelli.)

*B*efore you go on to fill out your final program worksheets,
we would like to remind you that no matter how wonderful or accomplished
a band or DJ you hire, and no matter how inexperienced you are, this is
your wedding. You owe it to yourself and your loved ones to make sure your
choices and style preferences are honored and expressed. With your
heart to guide you, and knowing you are giving the planning
all your love and imagination, we assure you—
your wedding music program will be magical.

FINAL PROGRAM WORKSHEETS

WEDDING PARTY PARTICIPANTS

Officiant _____

Parents of the Bride _____

_____

Parents of the Groom_____

_____

Grandparents of the Bride _____

_____

Grandparents of the Groom _____

_____

Other Parents (for blended families) _____

_____

Brothers and Sisters of the Bride_____

_____

Brothers and Sisters of the Groom _____

_____

Maid of Honor _____ Relationship _____

_____ Relationship _____

Best Man _____ Relationship _____

_____ Relationship _____

WEDDING PARTY PARTICIPANTS

Bridesmaids

Name_____

Name_____

Name_____

Name_____

Name_____

Name_____

Name_____

Name_____

Name_____

Flower Girl

_____

_____

Other Participants

_____

_____

_____

_____

_____

Groomsmen

_____

_____

_____

_____

_____

_____

_____

_____

_____

Ring Bearer

_____

_____

_____

_____

_____

_____

_____

PRELUDE MUSIC PROGRAM

Wedding Date: _____

Time: _____

_____

Location: _____

_____

Phone: _____

_____

Address: _____

_____

Setup Time: _____

_____

	Song/Music	*Soloist/Musician*

Prelude

Time: _____

Location: _____

Seating of Guests

Approximate Time: _____

Location: _____

PRELUDE MUSIC PROGRAM

	Song/Music	Soloist/Musician

Pre-Processional

Number of Participants: _____

Participants in Order of Entrance: _____

_____

_____

_____

_____

_____

_____

Special Considerations

_____

_____

_____

_____

_____

_____

_____

_____

_____

CEREMONY MUSIC PROGRAM

	Song/Music	Soloist/Musician

Processional

Number of Participants: _____

Participants in Order of Entrance (parents, grandparents, maid of honor, best man, bridesmaids,
    groomsmen, flower girl, ring bearer, etc.)

_____

_____

_____

_____

Ceremony

Invocation/Prayer _____

Solo/Song _____

Unity Candle_____

Recessional

_____

_____

_____

_____

_____

CEREMONY MUSIC PROGRAM

	Song/Music	Soloist/Musician

Interlude

Location: _____

_____

Approximate Time (How Long): _____

Receiving Line _____

_____

Must-Play Songs: _____

_____

_____

_____

_____

_____

General Selections: _____

_____

_____

_____

_____

_____

_____

LIST OF RECEPTION MUSIC PROGRAM EVENTS

In order of your personal preference, list your special moments under "Event/Participants" and the approximate time you and your bandleader or DJ and emcee arrange. List your final music and song selections under "Music/Song/Performer(s)." Here's a reminder of some special moments to choose from for your final program:

Grand entrance of bride and groom

May also include:

- Parents
- Best man and maid of honor
- Wedding party
- Other family

Welcoming special guests

- Out-of-towners
- Birthdays, etc.

Dances

- First dance
- Family/wedding party

- Change partners dance
- Group dances (see page 164 for specifics)
- Singles dances
- Ethnic dances
- Anniversary dance
- Dollar dance
- Last dance

Blessings, prayers, and toasts

- Wine/bread
- Best man and maid of honor
- Parents
- Friends
- Relatives

- Tributes to parents
- Bride and groom

Other special moments

- Cake cutting
- Bouquet toss
- Garter toss
  Groom removes garter?
- Circle of love
- Special performances
  Family, friends
- Family candle-lighting ceremony

RECEPTION MUSIC PROGRAM

Event / Participants:	Time:	Music / Song / Performer(s):

Emcee Announcements/Instructions:

Event / Participants:	Time:	Music / Song / Performer(s):

Emcee Announcements/Instructions:

RECEPTION MUSIC PROGRAM

Event/Participants:	Time:	Music/Song/Performer(s):

Emcee Announcements/Instructions:

Event/Participants:	Time:	Music/Song/Performer(s):

Emcee Announcements/Instructions:

RECEPTION MUSIC PROGRAM

Event/Participants:	Time:	Music/Song/Performer(s):

Emcee Announcements/Instructions:

Event/Participants:	Time:	Music/Song/Performer(s):

Emcee Announcements/Instructions:

RECEPTION MUSIC PROGRAM

Event / Participants:	Time:	Music / Song / Performer(s):

Emcee Announcements/Instructions:

Event / Participants:	Time:	Music / Song / Performer(s):

Emcee Announcements/Instructions:

RECEPTION MUSIC PROGRAM

Event/Participants:	*Time:*	*Music/Song/Performer(s):*

Emcee Announcements/Instructions:

Event/Participants:	*Time:*	*Music/Song/Performer(s):*

Emcee Announcements/Instructions:

Last-Minute Details — One Week Ahead

1. Call band or DJ and emcee to confirm all details:

    a. Weather forecasts and contingency arrangements.

    b. Last-minute changes in program or other details.

    c. Arrival time of musicians.

    d. Have they rehearsed special material agreed to?

    e. Make sure DJ and band (where applicable) have every CD you are planning to use in their hands.

    f. Make sure printouts of program are supplied to bandleader and band members, emcee, wedding coordinator (if applicable), and event planner at location; make copies for you and the groom.

    g. Ask a trusted friend or relative—not in the official wedding party—to be the one who will unofficially keep track of the program and to be a contact for the band for special requests, etc., so you are free during the wedding. (If you've hired good professionals, there should be little to do, but it will ease your mind to have your friend's support.)

2. Review the final program with your fiancé and family:

    a. Go over requests for songs, dances, toasts, and any special announcements or introductions.

    b. If a friend is going to act as DJ, it's a good idea to do a sound check to rehearse the sound system and set the proper volume levels in advance. The time to start fiddling around with a booming speaker or one that's practically inaudible is not when the ceremony is starting. Microphones that hiss and hum are annoying and can actually be harmful to the ear, so take care of these details well in advance if you are not having professionals handle this for you.

It's advisable to go over the sound system with the staff at the location (if applicable to your situation). Sound problems are distracting and will take away from the emotional impact of the moment.

Planning Tip

If a friend is acting as DJ, make sure to write down the title of each song, the album the song is on, and its track number on the CD when you write out your program list. Make a longer list than you think you can possibly use, and remember to list the songs you don't want played, as well.

Notes and Reminders

Notes and Reminders

We sincerely hope that reading *How to Set Your Wedding to Music* and using
this guide has been a joy. May music and song fill your lives forever
with lasting memories of the wedding of your dreams.
We wish you a beautiful wedding and a long
and happy journey together.

With love,

Barbara and Gloria

SONG LISTS BY CATEGORY

* Classical music albums are usually categorized by composer's name.

PRELUDE

Title	Artist	Album
"Adagio from Sonata in E-Flat"	—	Mozart*
"Aire in G" (Bach)	G. Sklerov	*For Your Wedding Ceremony* and *The Classical Collection*
"Andante from the 5th Symphony" (Beethoven)	G. Sklerov	*For Your Wedding Ceremony*
"Arabesque"	—	Debussy*

Title	Artist	Album
"Arioso" (Bach)	G. Sklerov	*For Your Wedding Ceremony* and *The Classical Collection*
"Brandenburg Concerto #4 in G" (allegro)	—	Bach*
"Clair de Lune"	—	Debussy*
"Greensleeves"	Renaissance Ensemble	*Set Your Wedding to Music* and *The Classical Collection*
"Largo"	—	Handel*
"Lascia Ch'io Pianga"	G. Sklerov	*For Your Wedding Ceremony* and *The Classical Collection*
"Minuet in G" (Mozart)	G. Sklerov	*For Your Wedding Ceremony* and *The Classical Collection*
"Nocturne in E-Flat, Op.9, No.2"	—	Chopin*
✈ Pachelbel's "Canon in D"	Ted Jacobs and David Chamberlin	*Set Your Wedding to Music* and *The Classical Collection*
"Pastoral Symphony"	—	Handel* *(Messiah)*
"Prelude in C" (Bach)	G. Sklerov	*For Your Wedding Ceremony*
"Preludes and Fugues"	—	*Bach for Organ*
"Prelude to 'The Afternoon of a Faun'"	—	Debussy*
"Someone to Watch over Me"	John Madatian	*Set Your Wedding to Music*
"So This Is Love" (instrumental)	David Hoffman Livingston	*Cinderella* (soundtrack)

Title	Artist	Album
"Through the Eyes of Love"	John Madatian	*Set Your Wedding to Music*
"Waltz from *Sleeping Beauty, Act I*"	—	Tchaikovsky*
"The Wedding Song (There Is Love)"	Laura Creamer	*Set Your Wedding to Music*

PRE-PROCESSIONAL/PROCESSIONAL

"Adagio from Sonata in E-Flat"	—	Mozart*
"Aire in G" (Bach)	G. Sklerov	*For Your Wedding Ceremony* and *The Classical Collection*
"Andante from the 5th Symphony" (Beethoven)	G. Sklerov	*For Your Wedding Ceremony*
"Arioso" (Bach)	G. Sklerov	*For Your Wedding Ceremony* and *The Classical Collection*
"Ave Maria" (Bach)	G. Sklerov	*For Your Wedding Ceremony* and *The Classical Collection*
"Bridal Chorus (Here Comes the Bride)"	Renaissance Ensemble	*Set Your Wedding to Music*, *For Your Wedding Ceremony*, and *The Classical Collection*
"Con Te Partiro" (Instrumental)	David Chamberlin	*Set Your Wedding to Music*
Elvira Madigan Theme	—	*Friends Forever*

Title	Artist	Album
"Erev Ba"	Shoshana Damari	*Israeli, Yiddish, Yemenite and Other Folk Songs*
"Four Seasons—Winter" (Vivaldi)	G. Sklerov	*For Your Wedding Ceremony*
"Gravement"	—	Bach*
"Greensleeves"	Renaissance Ensemble	*Set Your Wedding to Music* and *The Classical Collection*
"Jesu, Joy of Man's Desiring"	G. Sklerov	*For Your Wedding Ceremony* and *The Classical Collection*
"Lascia Ch'io Pianga"	G. Sklerov	*For Your Wedding Ceremony* and *The Classical Collection*
"Minuet in G" (Mozart)	G. Sklerov	*For Your Wedding Ceremony*
"One Hand, One Heart"	Cast	*West Side Story* (soundtrack)
⭑ Pachelbel's "Canon in D"	Renaissance Ensemble	*Set Your Wedding to Music* and *The Classical Collection*
"Processional/Te Deum"	—	Charpentier*
"Romance for String Quartet"	—	Mozart*
"Rondeau"—*Masterpiece Theatre* theme	Shoshana Damari	*Dream of the Manatee*
Theme from *Ice Castles*	John Madatian	*Set Your Wedding to Music*
"Trumpet Voluntary" (Clark) Prince of Denmark's March	G. Sklerov	*For Your Wedding Ceremony* and *The Classical Collection*

Ceremony/Unity Candle

Title	Artist	Album
"Always"	Atlantic Starr	*Greatest Hits*
"Amazing Grace"	Lari White	*Amazing Grace*
"Ave Maria"	—	Schubert*
"Because You Loved Me"	Celine Dion	*Falling into You*
"Coming Home"	Kimaya Seward	*Set Your Wedding to Music*
"Endless Love"	Lionel Ritchie and Diana Ross	*Truly: The Love Songs*
"Flesh of My Flesh"	Leon Patillo	*Songs 4 Life: Renew Your Heart!*
"From This Moment On"	Shania Twain and Bryan White	*Come On Over*
"Give Me Forever (I Do)"	John Tesh Ensemble	*Grand Passion for Music*
"Grow Old with Me"	Mary Chapin Carpenter	*Party Doll and Other Favorites*
"Here and Now"	Luther Vandross	*The Best of Luther Vandross*
"Household of Faith"	Steve and Anne Paynte	*Love Songs for Couples*
"I Believe in You and Me"	Whitney Houston	*The Preacher's Wife* (soundtrack)
"I Do"	Paul Brandt	*Calm Before the Storm*
"I Do (Cherish You)"	Mark Wills	*Wish You Were Here*

Title	Artist	Album
"I'll Always Be Right There"	Bryan Adams	*MTV Unplugged*
"It's Your Love"	Tim McGraw and Faith Hill	*Everywhere*
"Keeper of the Stars"	Tracy Byrd	*No Ordinary Man*
"Lord's Prayer"	—	Mallote*
"Love Knows No Wrong"	Lisa Frazier	*Set Your Wedding to Music*
"One Hand, One Heart"	Cast	*West Side Story* (soundtrack)
"The Wedding Song (There Is Love)"	Laura Creamer	*Set Your Wedding to Music*
"Wherever You Go"	David Haas	*When Love Is Found*
"You Light Up My Life"	LeAnn Rimes	*Inspirational Songs*
"Yours, Mine, and Ours"	Teresa James and David Chamberlin	*Yours, Mine, and Ours*

RECESSIONAL

Title	Artist	Album
"Chapel of Love"	The Moonlighters	*Set Your Wedding to Music*
"Four Seasons (Spring)"	—	Vivaldi*
"Hallelujah Chorus"	—	Handel*
"Hornpipe from *Water Music*" (Handel)	Festival Orchestra	*One Day/Your Day*
"La Rejoissance"	—	Handel*
"A Little Night Music"	—	Mozart*
"Rondeau"—*Masterpiece Theatre* theme	Shoshana Damari	*Dream of the Manatee*

Title	*Artist*	*Album*
"Trumpet Voluntary" (Clark)	G. Sklerov	*For Your Wedding Ceremony*
Prince of Denmark's March		and *The Classical Collection*
"Wedding March" (Mendelsson)	Rennaissance Ensemble	*For Your Wedding Ceremony,*
		Set Your Wedding to Music,
		and *The Classical Collection*

(See "Ethnic Choices" on page 169 for more ideas.)

Interlude

CLASSICAL

"Aire in G" (Bach)	G. Sklerov	*For Your Wedding Ceremony*
		and *The Classical Collection*
"Air—Sheep May Safely Graze"	—	Bach*
"Amen! Praise and Glory"	—	Peacock*
"Andante from the 5th Symphony" (Beethoven)	G. Sklerov	*For Your Wedding Ceremony*
"Arabesque"	—	Debussy*
"Ave Maria" (Bach)	G. Sklerov	*For Your Wedding Ceremony*
		and *The Classical Collection*
"Ave Maria" (Schubert)	—	*Songs for Your Wedding*
"The Call from Five Mystical Songs"	Vaughan Williams	Vaughan Williams*
"Clair de Lune"	—	Debussy*

Title	Artist	Album
"Greensleeves"	Renaissance Ensemble	*Set Your Wedding to Music* and *The Classical Collection*
"Hymn—Finlandia"	—	*Grieg**
"Jesu, Joy of Man's Desiring"	G. Sklerov	*For Your Wedding Ceremony* *The Classical Collection*
"Lascia Ch'io Pianga"	G. Sklerov	*For Your Wedding Ceremony* *The Classical Collection*
"Minuet in G"	G. Sklerov	*For Your Wedding Ceremony* *The Classical Collection*

CONTEMPORARY

Regardless of the style and setting of your wedding, many styles of contemporary music are appropriate for the interlude. Refer to some of our suggestions for soundtrack albums, ethnic choices, jazz, and swing. More than likely, some of your own favorite selections would be natural and appropriate choices. See the section about interludes in chapter 1 for more guidance.

COUPLE'S FIRST DANCE

| "After All" | Cher and Peter Cetera | *Peter Cetera's Collection* |
| "All I Ask of You" | Cast | *The Phantom of the Opera* (soundtrack) |

Title	Artist	Album
"All My Life"	Linda Ronstadt and Aaron Neville	*Cry Like a Rainstorm*
"All the Things You Are"	Tony Bennett	*Carnegie Hall*
"All the Way"	Celine Dion and Frank Sinatra	*All the Way* (new duet)
"Always"	—	Irving Berlin*
"Always and Forever"	Heatwave	*Too Hot to Handle*
"Amazed"	Lonestar	*I'm Already There*
"Annie's Song"	John Denver	*Back Home Again*
"As Time Goes By"	Cast	*Casablanca* (soundtrack)
"At Last"	Etta James	*Set Your Wedding to Music*
"Beautiful in My Eyes"	Joshua Kadison	*Premium Gold Collection*
"Because You Loved Me"	Molly Pasutti	*Set Your Wedding to Music*
"Breathe"	Faith Hill	*Breathe*
"Can't Help Falling in Love"	Elvis Presley	*Can't Help Falling in Love*
"Could I Have This Dance?"	Anne Murray	*An Intimate Evening*
"Endless Love"	Lionel Ritchie	*Truly: The Love Songs*
"Eternal Flame"	The Bangles	*Greatest Hits*
"Everything I Do"	Bryan Adams	*The Best of Me*
"Forever"	Kiss	*Hot in the Shade*
"Forever and Ever, Amen"	Randy Travis	*Greatest Hits, Vol. 2*
"For the First Time"	Kenny Loggins	*Yesterday, Today, Tomorrow*

Title	Artist	Album
"For You"	Kenny Lattimore	*Kenny Lattimore*
"For You I Will"	Monica	*The Boy Is Mine*
"From Here to Eternity"	Michael Petersen	*Michael Petersen*
"From This Moment On"	Shania Twain	*Come On Over*
"God Must Have Spent a Little More Time on You"	'N Sync	*'N Sync*
"Grow Old with Me"	Mary Chapin Carpenter	*Party Doll and Other Favorites*
"Have I Told You Lately That I Love You?"	Van Morrison	*Avalon Sunset*
"Have I Told You Lately That I Love You?"	Rod Stewart	*Vagabond Heart*
"How Sweet It Is"	James Taylor	*Best Live*
"The Gift"	Jim Brickman	*The Gift*
"I Believe in You and Me"	Whitney Houston	*The Preacher's Wife* (soundtrack)
"I Cross My Heart"	George Strait	*Pure Country* (soundtrack)
"I Don't Wanna Miss a Thing"	Aerosmith	*Armageddon* (soundtrack)
"I Give You My Heart"	John Berry	*Faces*
"I Just Fall in Love Again"	Anne Murray	*Greatest Hits, Vol. 1*
"I'll Always Be Right There"	Bryan Adams	*MTV Unplugged*
"I'll Always Love You"	Taylor Dayne	*Tell It to My Heart*
"I'll Be There"	Michael Jackson and Mariah Carey	*Mariah Carey #1s*
"I'll Stand by You"	The Pretenders	*Last of the Independents*

Title	Artist	Album
"I Love the Way You Love Me"	John Michael Montgomery	*Greatest Hits*
"I've Finally Found Someone"	Barbra Streisand and Bryan Adams	*Eighteen 'Til I Die*
"I'm Your Angel"	R. Kelly and Celine Dion	*These Are Special*
"In My Life"	The Beatles	*Rubber Soul*
"In Your Eyes"	Peter Gabriel	*So*
"It Had to Be You"	Harry Connick Jr.	*When Harry Met Sally* (soundtrack)
"It's Your Love"	Tim McGraw and Faith Hill	*Greatest Hits*
"I Will If You Will"	John Berry	*Faces*
"Just the Way You Look Tonight"	Tony Bennett	*My Best Friend's Wedding* (soundtrack)
"Just You and I"	Crystal Gayle and Eddie Rabbit	*Greatest Hits* (Eddie Rabbit)
"Love Knows No Wrong"	Lisa Frazier	*Set Your Wedding to Music*
"Love of a Lifetime"	Firehouse	*Good Acoustics*
"Me and You"	Kenny Chesney	*Me and You*
"Now and Forever"	Richard Marx	*Greatest Hits*
"The Power of Love"	Celine Dion	*Colour of My Love*
"Something"	The Beatles	*Abbey Road*

Title	Artist	Album
"Something About the Way You Look Tonight"	Elton John	*The Big Picture*
"Somewhere Out There"	Linda Ronstadt and James Ingram	*An American Tail* (soundtrack)
"Still the One"	Shania Twain	*Come On Over*
"To Make You Feel My Love"	Garth Brooks	*Hope Floats* (soundtrack)
"Tonight I Celebrate My Love for You"	Roberta Flack and Peabo Bryson	*Collection* (Peabo Bryson)
"True Companion"	Marc Cohn	*True Companion*
"Truly, Madly, Deeply"	Savage Garden	*Savage Garden*
"Two Hearts—One Love"	Kimaya and Monte Seward	*Set Your Wedding to Music*
"Unchained Melody"	The Righteous Brothers	*Best of the Righteous Brothers*
"Unforgettable"	Natalie Cole	*Unforgettable*
"Until I Was Loved by You"	Stan Bush	*Set Your Wedding to Music*
"Vision of Love"	Mariah Carey	*Mariah Carey #1s*
"What a Wonderful World"	Louis Armstrong	*An American Icon*
"When a Man Loves a Woman"	Michael Bolton	*Greatest Hits, 1985–95*
"When I Fall in Love"	Celine Dion and Clive Griffin	*Colour of My Love*
"When I Needed You Most"	Kimaya Seward	*Yours, Mine, and Ours*
"When You Say Nothing at All"	Alison Krauss	*Now That I've Found You*

Title	Artist	Album
"A Whole New World"	Peabo Bryson and Regina Bell	*Aladdin* (soundtrack)
"Wind Beneath My Wings"	Bette Midler	*Beaches* (soundtrack)
"You Are So Beautiful"	Joe Cocker	*Classics*
"You're the Inspiration"	Chicago	*Chicago 17*
"Your Love Amazes Me"	John Berry	*Greatest Hits*

FATHER-DAUGHTER DANCE

Title	Artist	Album
"Because You Loved Me"	Celine Dion	*Falling into You*
"Because You Loved Me"	Molly Pasutti	*Set Your Wedding to Music*
"Butterfly Kisses"	Bob Carlisle	*Butterfly Kisses (Shades of Grace)*
"Can You Feel the Love Tonight?"	Elton John	*The Lion King* (soundtrack)
"Daddy's Girl"	Peter Cetera	*Solitude/Solitaire*
"Daddy's Hands"	Holly Dunn	*Milestones: Greatest Hits*
"Daddy's Little Girl"	Kippi Brannon	*Butterfly Kisses*
"Father's Eyes"	Amy Grant	*My Father's Eyes*
"Have I Told You Lately That I Love You?"	Van Morrison	*Avalon Sunset*
"Have I Told You Lately That I Love You?"	Rod Stewart	*Vagabond Heart*

Title	*Artist*	*Album*
"I'll Be There"	Michael Jackson and Mariah Carey	*Mariah Carey #1s*
"Isn't She Lovely?"	Stevie Wonder	*Songs in the Key of Life*
"Just the Way You Are"	Billy Joel	*The Stranger*
"Landslide"	Fleetwood Mac	*Fleetwood Mac*
"Love of My Life"	Carly Simon	*Clouds in My Coffee*
"Lullaby"	Billy Joel	*River of Dreams*
"My Girl"	The Temptations	*My Girl*
"My Little Girl"	Steve Kirwan	*Yours, Mine, and Ours*
"Sunrise, Sunset"	Steve Kirwan	*Set Your Wedding to Music*
"Thank Heaven for Little Girls"	Maurice Chevalier	*Gigi* (soundtrack)
"Through the Years"	Kenny Rogers	*20 Greatest Hits*
"Times of Your Life"	Paul Anka	*Classic Hits*
"Unforgettable"	Natalie Cole	*Unforgettable*
"The Way You Look Tonight"	Frank Sinatra	*The Very Best of Frank Sinatra*
"What a Wonderful World"	Louis Armstrong	*An American Icon*
"Wind Beneath My Wings"	Bette Midler	*Beaches* (soundtrack)
"You Are So Beautiful"	Joe Cocker	*Joe Cocker Classics, Vol. 4*
"You're My Hero"	Teresa James	*Yours, Mine, and Ours*
"A Whole New World"	Peabo Bryson and Regina Bell	*Aladdin* (soundtrack)

Mother-Son Dance

Title	Artist	Album
"Because You Loved Me"	Celine Dion	*Falling into You*
"Because You Loved Me"	Molly Pasutti	*Set Your Wedding to Music*
"Blessed"	Elton John	*Love Songs*
"First Time Ever I Saw Your Face"	Roberta Flack	*First Take*
"Greatest Love of All"	Whitney Houston	*Whitney*
"Have I Told You Lately That I Love You?"	Van Morrison	*Avalon Sunset*
"Have I Told You Lately That I Love You?"	Rod Stewart	*Vagabond Heart*
"I Am Your Child"	Barry Manilow	*The Complete Collection*
"In My Life"	The Beatles	*All-Time Favorites*
"In This Life"	Bette Midler	*Bette of Roses*
"In Your Eyes"	David Chamberlin	*Yours, Mine, and Ours*
"I Will Always Love You"	Whitney Houston	*The Bodyguard* (soundtrack)
"I Wish You Love"	Natalie Cole	*Take a Look*
"The Man You've Become"	Molly Pasutti	*Yours, Mine, and Ours*
"Sunrise, Sunset"	Steve Kirwan	*Set Your Wedding to Music*
"Through the Years"	Kenny Rogers	*20 Greatest Hits*
"Wind Beneath My Wings"	Bette Midler	*Beaches* (soundtrack)
"You're the Inspiration"	Chicago	*Chicago 17*

Family Dances

Title	Artist	Album
"Because You Loved Me"	Celine Dion	*Falling into You*
"Because You Loved Me"	Molly Pasutti	*Set Your Wedding to Music*
"Blessed"	Elton John	*Love Songs*
"Coming Home"	Kimaya Seward	*Set Your Wedding to Music*
"Forever in Love"	Kenny G	*Breathless*
"Have I Told You Lately That I Love You?"	Van Morrison	*Avalon Sunset*
"Have I Told You Lately That I Love You?"	Rod Stewart	*Vagabond Heart*
"He Ain't Heavy, He's My Brother"	The Hollies	*All-Time Greatest Hits*
"In My Life"	The Beatles	*Red Album*
"Lean on Me"	Bill Withers	*Greatest Hits*
"May Each Day"	Andy Williams	*Greatest Hits*
"Memories"	Elvis Presley	*Elvis' Gold Records, Vol. 5*
"Moonlight Memories of You"	Barry Manilow	*Barry Manilow*
"Stand by Me"	Ben E. King	*Anthology*
"Sunrise, Sunset"	Cast	*Fiddler on the Roof*
"Sunrise, Sunset"	Steve Kirwan	*Set Your Wedding to Music*
"Thanks Again, Family"	Ricky Scaggs	*Comin' Home to Stay*
"They Can't Take That Away from Me"	Frank Sinatra and Natalie Cole	*Duets*

Title	Artist	Album
"Through the Years"	Kenny Rogers	*20 Greatest Hits*
"Times of Your Life"	Paul Anka	*30th Anniversary Anthology*
"Unforgettable"	Natalie Cole	*Unforgettable*
"The Way You Look Tonight"	Frank Sinatra	*The Columbia Years*
"We Are Family"	Sister Sledge	*We Are Family*
"We Are One"	Cast	*The Lion King* (soundtrack)
"What a Wonderful World"	Louis Armstrong	*An American Icon*
"Wind Beneath My Wings"	Bette Midler	*Experience the Divine*
"Yours, Mine, and Ours"	Teresa James and David Chamberlin	*Yours, Mine, and Ours*

SONGS FOR THE WEDDING PARTY

"All My Life"	Jojo and K. C.	*Love Always*
"Because You Loved Me"	Celine Dion	*Falling into You*
"Because You Loved Me"	Molly Pasutti	*Set Your Wedding to Music*
"Can You Feel the Love Tonight?"	Elton John	*The Lion King* (soundtrack)
"Celebration"	Kool and the Gang	*Celebrate*
"Circle of Life"	Elton John	*The Lion King* (soundtrack)
"Endless Love"	Lionel Ritchie and Diana Ross	*Truly: The Love Songs*
"Everybody Have Fun Tonight"	Wang Chung	*Everybody Wang Chung Tonight*

Title	Artist	Album
"Friends"	Elton John	*Rare Masters*
"Friends"	Michael W. Smith	*Change Your World*
"Friends in Low Places"	Garth Brooks	*No Fences*
"From This Moment On"	Shania Twain and Bryan White	*Come On Over*
"I Do (Cherish You)"	98 Degrees	*98 Degrees and Rising*
"I Do (Cherish You)"	Mark Wills	*Mark Wills*
"I'll Be There for You"	The Rembrandts	*Friends* (soundtrack)
"In Your Eyes"	Peter Gabriel	*So*
"It's Your Love"	Tim McGraw and Faith Hill	*Everywhere*
"I Will Be Your Friend"	Amy Grant	*Behind the Eyes*
"Shower the People"	James Taylor	*Best Live*
"That's What Friends Are For"	Dionne Warwick	*Friends*
"To Make You Feel My Love"	Garth Brooks	*Hope Floats* (soundtrack)
"Truly, Madly, Deeply"	Savage Garden	*Savage Garden*
"We Are Family"	Sister Sledge	*We Are Family*
"What a Wonderful World"	Louis Armstrong	*An American Icon*
"Wind Beneath My Wings"	Bette Midler	*Beaches* (soundtrack)
"You're Still the One"	Shania Twain	*Come On Over*
"You've Got a Friend"	James Taylor	*Greatest Hits*

CAKE CUTTING

Title	Artist	Album
"All My Life"	Jojo and K. C.	*Love Always*
"Better Be Good to Me"	Tina Turner	*Simply the Best*
"Chapel of Love"	Moonlighters	*Set Your Wedding to Music*
"Eat It"	"Weird" Al Yankovic	*Greatest Hits*
"From This Moment On"	Shania Twain and Bryan White	*Come On Over*
"Hit Me with Your Best Shot"	Pat Benatar	*All Fired Up . . .*
"How Sweet It Is (to Be Loved By You)"	James Taylor	*Greatest Hits*
"I Don't Wanna Miss a Thing"	Aerosmith	*Armageddon* (soundtrack)
"I Got You Babe"	Sonny and Cher	*The Beat Goes On*
"In Your Eyes"	Peter Gabriel	*So*
"I Swear"	John Michael Montgomery	*Kickin' It Up*
"It Had to Be You"	Harry Connick Jr.	*When Harry Met Sally* (soundtrack)
"It's Your Love"	Faith Hill and Tim McGraw	*Everywhere*
"Love and Marriage"	Frank Sinatra	*Best of Sinatra*
"Recipe for Love"	Harry Connick Jr.	*We Are in Love*

Title	Artist	Album
"Sugar, Sugar"	The Archies	*Sugar, Sugar (limited edition)*
"That's Amore"	Dean Martin	*All-Time Greatest Hits*
"This Guy's in Love with You"	Herb Alpert	*Foursider*
"Unchained Melody"	The Righteous Brothers	*Best of the Righteous Brothers*
"Unforgettable"	Nat King Cole	*Best of Nat King Cole*
"The Way You Look Tonight"	Frank Sinatra	*The Columbia Years*
"When I'm Sixty-Four"	The Beatles	*Sgt. Pepper's Lonely Hearts Club Band*

BOUQUET TOSS

"Chapel of Love"	Moonlighters	*Set Your Wedding to Music*
"Everything's Coming Up Roses"	Michael Feinstein	*Jule Styne Songbook*
"Girls' Night Out"	The Judds	*Why Not Me?*
"I Enjoy Being a Girl"	Doris Day and Peggy Lee	*I Have Dreamed Greatest Hits*
"I Feel Pretty"	Julie Andrews	*A Little Bit of Broadway*
"Isn't She Lovely?"	Stevie Wonder	*Songs in the Key of Life*
"Man, I Feel Like a Woman"	Shania Twain	*Come On Over*
"Oh Pretty Woman"	Roy Orbison	*The All-Time Greatest Hits of Roy Orbison*
"Why Not Me?"	The Judds	*Why Not Me?*

GARTER TOSS

Title	Artist	Album
"Another One Bites the Dust"	Queen	Crown Jewels
"Bad Boys"	Inner Circle	Identified
"Curly Shuffle"	Jump 'N the Saddle	Dr. Demento: 25th Anniversary Collection
"Do Ya Think I'm Sexy?"	Rod Stewart	Blondes Have More Fun
"Fever"	Peggy Lee	The Best of Peggy Lee
"Freak Me"	Silk	Lose Control
"Gimme All Your Lovin'"	ZZ Top	Eliminator
"Guys Do It All the Time"	Mindy McCready	Ten Thousand Angels
"Heaven"	Bryan Adams	Reckless
"Hungry Eyes"	Eric Carmen	Definitive Collection
"I'm Too Sexy"	Right Said Fred	1992 Billboard Greatest Hits
"Kiss"	Prince	Parade
"Legs"	ZZ Top	Eliminator
"Let's Get It On"	Marvin Gaye	Let's Get It On
"Macho Man"	Village People	Macho Man
"Oh Pretty Woman"	Roy Orbison	The All-Time Greatest Hits of Roy Orbison
"Oh Yeah"	Yello	Essentials

Title	Artist	Album
"Rub You the Right Way"	Johnny Gill	*Johnny Gill*
"Shameless"	Garth Brooks	*Double Live*
"Simply Irresistible"	Robert Palmer	*Rock 'n' Roll Relix*
"The Stripper"	David Rose	*Bachelor Pad*
"Theme from *Mission: Impossible*"	Danny Elfman	*Mission: Impossible* (soundtrack)
"U Can't Touch This"	M. C. Hammer	*Greatest Hits*
"Unchained Melody"	The Righteous Brothers	*Best of the Righteous Brothers*
"Wild Thing"	The Troggs	*The Best of the Troggs*
"You Can Leave Your Hat On"	Joe Cocker	*The Full Monty* (soundtrack)
"You Sexy Thing"	Hot Chocolate	*The Full Monty* (soundtrack)

GROUP DANCES

Anniversaries—Call up couples to dance married five, ten, fifteen, twenty years, until you find the couple married the longest.

Brunettes with blondes/redheads

Bunny Hop

Conga line

"Electric Slide"

Glasses with no glasses

"Hands Up"

Hora

Locals with out-of-towners

Older with younger

Sadie Hawkins (girls ask the guys)

The smallest with the tallest

Switch partners

Those who know each other from school

Virginia Reel

"YMCA"

CHRISTIAN WEDDING SONGS

Title	*Artist*	*Album*
"Across the Miles"	Paul Alan	*Nouveaux Beginnings*
"All of Me"	Stryper	*To Hell with the Devil*
"Arise My Love"	Michael Card	*The Way of Wisdom*
"Babe"	Scott Wesley Brown	*Signature*
"Beautiful"	Plankeye	*Commonwealth*
"Bonded Together"	Twila Paris	*Same Girl*
"Bride's Song 1984"	Riki Michelle	*Big Big Town*
"Bridge Across the Water"	Taylor Rhodes	*Nouveaux Beginnings*
"Cross My Heart"	Michael W. Smith	*Go West Young Man*

Title	Artist	Album
"Doubly Good to You"	Amy Grant	*Straight Ahead*
"Dream in My Life"	King's X	*King's X*
"Edge of the Dream"	White Heart	*Emergency Broadcast*
"Eternity"	Brian Doerksen	*Jesus Alone*
"Fallin' in Love"	Shaded Red	*Shaded Red*
"For You"	Michael W. Smith	*Go West Young Man*
"Go There with You"	Steven Curtis Chapman	*Great Adventure*
"Hand in Hand"	DeGarmo and Key	*The Pledge*
"Heirlooms"	Amy Grant	*Christmas Album*
"Here and Now"	Phil Keaggy	*Way Back Home*
"Honestly"	Stryper	*To Hell with the Devil*
"Household of Faith"	Steve Green	*For God and God Alone*
"How Beautiful"	Twila Paris	*Cry for the Desert*
"I Do"	Phil and Brenda Nicholas	*More Than Music*
"I Found Love"	Guardian	*Miracle Mile*
"I Found Myself in You"	Clay Crosse	*Time to Believe*
"I'll Give"	Smalltown Poets	*Smalltown Poets*
"I'm Committed to You"	Steve Camp	*Talking Heaven*
"I Will Be Here"	Steven Chapman	*More to This Life*
"I Wish"	Billy Sprague	*La Vie*
"Jesus in Your Eyes"	Julie Miller	*Orphans and Angels*
"Love"	Petra	*Beyond Belief*

Title	Artist	Album
"Love Divine"	Phil Keaggy	*Crimson and Blue*
"Love I Know"	PFR	*Great Lengths*
"Love Never Fails"	Servant	*Swimming*
"Love of My Life"	Sheila Walsh	*For a Time Like This*
"Love Song"	Third Day	*Third Day*
"Maybe Tomorrow"	Nouveaux	*And This Is How I Feel*
"Melody's Song"	Keith Green	*Prodigal Son*
"My Promise"	Tourniquet	*Nouveaux Beginnings; Vanishing Lessons*
"Never Say Good-bye"	Guardian	*Fire*
"Nowhere Else"	77s	*Sticks and Stones*
"One at Heart"	Servant	*Light Maneuvers*
"Open Arms"	Amy Grant	*Straight Ahead*
"Over and Over"	Annie Herring	*There's a Stirring*
"Perfect Union"	Mathew Ward	*Fade to White*
"Say Once More"	Amy Grant	*Lead Me On*
"Security"	Leon Patillo	*The Sky's the Limit*
"She's My Angel"	Dreamer	*Full Metal Racket*
"Since I Found You"	Matthew Ward	*Fortress*
"Still in Love"	East to West	*North of the Sky*
"Take My Hand, Love"	Between Thieves	*Between Thieves*
"Thy Word"	Amy Grant	*Straight Ahead*

Title	Artist	Album
"Time"	Rachel Rachel	*You Oughta Know by Now*
"Together as One"	Stryper	*Soldiers Under Command*
"True Friend"	Twila Paris	*For Every Heart*
"The Vow"	Geoff Moore	*Home Run*
"The Wedding"	Michael Card	*Scandalon*
"Wedding Prayer"	Glen Kasier	*All My Days*
"The Wedding Song (There Is Love)"	Laura Creamer	*Set Your Wedding to Music*
"Whatever It Takes"	Amy Grant	*House of Love*
"Why Don't We?"	Guardian	*Swing Swang Swung*
"Wonderful"	Bleach	*Space*
"You and I"	Guardian	*Miracle Mile*

SOUNDTRACK ALBUMS — A FEW SUGGESTIONS

Beauty and the Beast

City of Angels

The English Patient

Heart of the Ocean (film music of James Horner)

Movie Memories (John Williams)

Out of Africa

Saturday Night Fever (great seventies disco hits)

Cinderella

Dangerous Beauty

Fantasia (Walt Disney)

Ice Castles

My Best Friend's Wedding

Phantom of the Opera

Sleepless in Seattle

Somewhere in Time   *When Harry Met Sally*
                                                            (featuring Harry Connick Jr.)
You Must Remember This (classic film scores of Franz Waxman and Max Steiner)

ETHNIC CHOICES

BRAZILIAN

"Brazil"   "Corcovado"   "Desafinado"

"Girl from Ipanema"   "How Insensitive"   "Meditation (Pensativa)"

"O Grande Amor"   "One Note Samba"   "Someone to Light Up
                                                                    My Life"

"Triste"   "Wave"

IRISH

"Danny Boy"   "Did Your Mother Come   "Finnegan's Wake"
                                    from Ireland?"

"Galway Bay"   "Gary Owen"   "Irish Washerwoman"

"It's a Long Way to Tipperary" "Miller's Reel"   "Mother Machree"

"My Wild Irish Rose"   "Peg of My Heart"   "Sweet Rosie O'Grady"

"Too-Rah-Loo-Rah"   "The Wearin' of the Green"   "When Irish Eyes Are Smiling"

ITALIAN

"Al Di La"

"Arriverderci Roma"

"Mala Femmena"

"Oh, Marie"

"O Sole Mio"

"Santa Lucia"

"Sorrento Volare"

"Tartantella"

"Volare"

JEWISH

"Bashana"

"Dodi Li"

"Erev Shel Shoshanim"

"Fiddler on the Roof" (title song)

"Hava Nagila"

"If I Were a Rich Man"

"Mazel Tov Hevenu"

"Raisins and Almonds"

"Shalom Man"

"Simon Tov"

"Sunrise, Sunset"

"To Life"

"Tsena Tsena"

"Y'Rushalayim"

SPANISH

"China" (Tito Puente)

"Cielito Lindo"

"Cuban Pete" (Mambo Kings)

"Decidete" (Orquesta Aragon)

"Es Muy Tarde" (Susie Hansen)

"Granada"

"Green Eyes"

"Guantanamera" (traditional)

"La Golondrina"

"Maria Elena"

"Mexican Hat Dance"

"Oye Como Va" (Tito Puente)

"Spanish Eyes"

MISCELLANEOUS ETHNIC

"A Felicidad"

"Beer Barrel Polka"

"Begin the Beguine" (rumba)

"Dindi"

"Ela a Carioca"

"Helena Polka"

"Liechensteiner" "Melody of Love" "Miserlou"

"Once I Loved" "Pennsylvania Polka" "Samba de Orly"

"Summer Samba" "Yellow Bird" (calypso) "Zorba the Greek"

MISCELLANEOUS ETHNIC WEDDING ALBUMS

Celtic Wedding by the Chieftains (The Chieftains) *The Golden Gate Gypsy Orchestra*

Greek Traditional Music Collection *Irish Wedding Party*

Mombassa Wedding Special *Music for a Jewish Wedding*

Polish Wedding (Luis Bacalov) *The Traveling Jewish Wedding*

Wedding Songs, Vols. 4–18

RHYTHMIC CHOICES

ROCK—'50S AND '60S

"Dancing in the Street" "Evil Ways" "Fever"

"Get Ready" "Gimme Some Lovin'" "Good Lovin'"

"Heard It Through the Grapevine" "Hold On, I'm Coming" "I Saw Her Standing There"

"Johnny B. Goode" "Jumpin' Jack Flash" "Kansas City"

"Knock on Wood" "La Bamba" "Long Tall Sally"

"Midnight Hour" "Mony, Mony" "Mustang Sally"

"My Girl" "Rock Around the Clock" "Rockin' Robin"

"Shout" "Signed, Sealed, Delivered" "Sittin' on the Dock of the Bay"

"Soul Man" "Stand by Me" "Sugar Pie Honey Bunch"

"Twist and Shout" "Walk Right In" "Workin' My Way Back to You"

SALSA (in English)

"Beautiful Maria" (Mambo Kings) "I Want to Love You" (Angel Lopez)

"Livin' la Vida Loca" (Ricky Martin) "To Be with You" (Joe Cuba)

"Was I Surprised" (Carabali)

SWING

Fast

"Anything Goes" "I Got Rhythm" "In the Mood"

"Kansas City" "Lady Be Good" "Love Is Here to Stay"

"Mack the Knife" "Night Train" "One O'Clock Jump"

"Perdido" "Stompin' at the Savoy" "'S Wonderful"

"Take the 'A' Train" "The Way You Look Tonight"

Slow

"April in Paris" "Blue Moon" "I Left My Heart in San Francisco"

"I Remember You" "It Had to Be You" "Just in Time"

"Moonglow" (theme from *Picnic*) "Moonlight Serenade" "The More I See You"

"New York, New York" "On a Clear Day" "Satin Doll"

"Sentimental Journey"

General Wedding Albums

The Complete Wedding Album (Telarc Records) (two-CD set of classical music featuring full symphony orchestrations and themes from four films)

The Country Wedding Album (various artists)

For Your Wedding Ceremony (orchestrated classical ceremony music)

Les Yeux Noir (French and klezmer) (an international hit album)

My Best Friend's Wedding (soundtrack)

Set Your Wedding to Music (various artists, instrumentals, and vocals for special moments of the reception and ceremony)

A Time for Us (various artists)

Ultimate Wedding Collection—Danny Wright (piano instrumentals)

The Wedding Collection (two-CD set of classical and pop soundalike versions)

The Wedding Singer (soundtrack)

Yours, Mine, and Ours (seven new songs for father-daughter and mother-son dances, stepparents, mentors, and family unity, plus instrumental tracks)

We've found that the best Web sites for looking up specific music selections by song, artist, or category are cdnow.com, buymusic.com, and allmusic.com. With these three sites, you can look up titles and find out where to buy virtually all recorded music currently available. Also check out thesource.com or prodj.com, the largest distributors of dance music for DJs.

SAMPLE ENTERTAINMENT CONTRACT

This agreement for entertainment is made this _____ day of _____, _____, by and between (CLIENT) and ABC MUSIC (hereafter known as the COMPANY), under the following mutually agreed conditions:

OCCASION:

Wedding of _____and

_____

DATE OF WEDDING: _____

LOCATION: _____

TIME: _____

PROGRAM:

1. Ceremony: Keyboard and flute—one hour

2. Cocktails (interlude): Keyboard and sax for cocktails—one hour

3. Reception: Six-piece studio band—four hours

TOTAL FEE: _____

RETAINER (20%): _____

DATE BALANCE DUE: Five working days prior to event (by cash, cashier's check, or money order)

I. OPTIONS:

    a.   Client may add additional musicians to band @ _____ per musician.

    b.   Client may add continuous music (no breaks whatsoever) @ additional _____ per man.

    c.   Specialty entertainment and/or other special services to be covered under separate agreement at discretion of client (vocalists, dancers, etc.).

2.   OVERTIME: Should client wish to engage performer(s) for a period of time exceeding the above designated hours, subject to performer(s)'s availability, the performer(s) may be engaged for no less than half-hour segments, payable at the following rates:

    a.   Musicians/vocalists/dancers: _____ per performer/per half-hour

    b.   Disc jockey/master of ceremonies: _____ per performer/per half-hour

Overtime charges are payable to band leader at end of event.

3. METHOD OF PAYMENT: Cash, cashier's check, or money order, drawn of banks located in the counties of _____ or _____, state of _____, are acceptable. Out-of-area documents or credit cards shall not be accepted. Payments are to be made payable to _____.

Final balance is due and payable no later than five working days prior to date of event.

4. EARLY SETUP: Setup is to be completed fifteen minutes prior to official start time. If client requires group to have equipment set up earlier than fifteen minutes before, it shall be considered "overtime" and be charged at the same rates as scheduled above. Early setup charge shall be added to the final balance and is due and payable with final balance.

5. OUTDOOR SETUP: Client shall provide the following for all segments of the event that shall take place outdoors: appropriate shade/awning cover during daylight performance, heaters and adequate lighting of band and dance floor for evening performances, stage or raised platform for band setup (dimension of platform to be determined by band size), adequate electrical amperage (forty amps for band—two dedicated twenty-amp circuits) and reasonable access to outlets (less than thirty feet) at all locations where amplified music is to be provided. At client's request, company will quote on provision of supplemental electrical wiring, lighting, and decor services under separate agreement.

6. LOAD-IN SURCHARGE: Client must advise company of unusual load-in circumstances, including excessive stairs, long distances between location for unloading vehicles and setup location, and any other situation or obstruction that may require extraordinary effort to be made for setup. There shall be a surcharge of $25 per band member ($50 per disc jockey) for any location that requires

company personnel to carry equipment up or down more than six steps or transport equipment by hand over a distance of more than fifty yards.

7. CANCELLATION POLICY: Retainers are nonrefundable under all circumstances. Written cancellations received by company via certified mail six months or more prior to date of event shall qualify for a credit of 50 percent of paid retainer, which may only be applied toward a future entertainment agreement directly between client and company of similar or greater value.

8. GRATUITIES: To answer our many clients who have asked, we suggest an optional 10 percent gratuity to the band leader or disc jockey at the conclusion of the affair.

9. This agreement shall become effective upon receipt by company of a signed copy of the agreement within seven days of the date thereof. The retainer, which is nonrefundable, must accompany the signed copy of this agreement. In the case of extreme emergency, such as earthquake, automobile accident, illness, disaster, or other unavoidable cause, company shall attempt to replace performing musical group members collectively or individually but shall in no event be responsible or held liable for any such proven absences. Should company not receive a signed copy of this agreement, accompanied by the retainer, within seven days of the date thereof, the terms and conditions of this agreement shall not become effective and company shall be free to enter into any agreement with other persons in regard to the services to be performed agreed upon herein.

CLIENT: _____

REPRESENTING: _____

ADDRESS: _____

CITY, STATE, ZIP: _____

TELEPHONE—RES.: _____ BUS.:_____

AGREED AND ACCEPTED BY CLIENT: _____

DATE: _____

BY COMPANY: _____

DATE _____

CONTRACT OVERVIEW

This contract is pretty standard for top bands. Most paragraphs are self-explanatory. Notice that the method of payment set out in Number 3 does not allow for credit card payments. If your band or music service company does take credit cards, it's a good idea to pay by card if your credit card company offers a buyer's protection plan. Call your credit card's customer service department for complete information. Number 4, a provision for setup to be completed fifteen minutes before the "official" start time, is standard. This should allow for music to be playing when the first guests arrive.

Number 5 refers to the additional equipment needed for an outdoor setting. You can discuss this with the staff at your location (hotel, catering establishment, etc.) and see what they provide. More than likely, they will be prepared for weddings held outdoors on their grounds. Your job is to designate the person to have all the equipment there on time and in good working order. By all means, make a separate agreement in writing with the band and/or hotel regarding the equipment for which they are to be responsible.

Number 6 is another standard provision. Cartage of equipment for difficult access or with more than five or six stairs runs into money. For a six-piece band, $25 per musician ($150) is not unreasonable.

Number 7 shows how careful the band is about protecting its scheduling time by requiring a 50 percent forfeiture for cancellation, even six months in advance. Don't sign until you are sure, and never sign if you feel pressured.

Number 9 is often called a "Force Majeure," or "Act of God," clause. No band or hotel wants to assume responsibility or absorb the total loss in cases of extreme emergency. Consider wedding insurance for your peace of mind. This will cover you in case an emergency requires a cancellation or postponement. Call 800-ENGAGED for details.

Additional clauses may be added to the contract to reflect such items as designated musicians, acceptable substitutes, etc. (See the Music Contract Checklist on page 59.)

Appendix C

WEDDING WEB SITES

- digitalbliss.com—Interactive wedding announcement service. Individual Web sites keep family, friends, and guests up-to-the-minute regarding wedding and reception plans, hotel accommodations, maps, and driving directions. Customer care reps update your site as often as you like at no added cost to you.

- marthastewart.com—Click on Weddings on Martha's Web site for in-depth information as well as shopping via Martha by Mail. Check the site for bulletin boards and live discussions.

- master-plans.com—Online wedding albums. Share your wedding day with friends and family around the world—from your computer. Order photos online. Keep track of guest lists, airport information, hotels, etc., and RSVP online.

- modernbride.com—Another fine wedding Web site; in-depth information with easy-to-maneuver pages for your wedding planning; great for online wedding chats.

- theknot.com—Offers a bridal registry service, personal wedding pages, wedding chats, message boards, ideas, a bridal search for wedding gifts, and advice. (The Knot is famous for its fine wedding book, *Complete Guide to Weddings in the Real World.*)

- ultimatewedding.com—A great site—easy to maneuver, comprehensive, all in a user-friendly format. An interesting collection of stores and shops with customer service and support online or direct by telephone. Popular brand-name products at competitive prices are presented in a familiar shopping-mall atmosphere.

- weddingchannel.com—A one-stop destination for engaged couples and their friends, family, and acquaintances. Offers many wedding-related services, online registry, personalization features, and online travel planning. Type in your city and you will get free referrals for musicians and other vendors in your local area.

- weddingpages.com—You can click to wedding vendors and bridal shows in your local area.

- weddingscoop.com—Your own wedding Web site. You can establish an up-to-date calendar of your wedding-related events, with links to your gift registry, an online RSVP service, and family photos. This site is great for keeping out-of-town guests up-to-the-minute on important wedding information.

TO ORDER WEDDING CDS, BOOKS, AND SHEET MUSIC

- allmusic.com
- bn.com (Barnes and Noble)
- borders.com
- cdnow.com
- sheetmusic.com
- thesource.com
- weddingmusiccentral.com

- amazon.com
- booksamillion.com
- buy.com
- ebay.com
- shop.com
- towerrecords.com

BRIDAL SHOWS

- The Great Bridal Expo, sponsored by *Modern Bride,* is a national bridal show that travels to a number of cities all over the country during the year; with the sponsorship of *Modern Bride* magazine, it has a highly regarded reputation.
- brideworld.com—We personally attended one of their shows in Southern California and were impressed by the high quality of vendors and the friendly atmosphere.
- Theweddingchannel.com, theknot.com, and ultimatewedding.com all have links to bridal shows in your area.

Wedding Referral Services

- The Association for Wedding Professionals International, afwpi.com, offers a free referral service and directory of members.

Wedding Music Services

To find a band or DJ in your area, you can start by clicking on the links on any one of the wedding Web sites, such as theknot.com, weddingchannel.com, and ultimatewedding.com. They will have direct links into your city or area and will supply you with a list of local musicians, soloists, and DJs. In addition, we've listed some other sources to look into that may be in your region.

- *Awesome Entertainment* of Southern California is a mobile music service run by Mark Thomas, national director of the PDJA (Professional DJ Association) in Los Angeles. Their main business is wedding-related DJ services, but they also supply all forms of entertainment, from steel bands to Elvis look-alikes. They provide emcees and coordinate complete affairs and will send music samples to choose from. weddingwarehouse.com; 800-430-4487.

- *1-800-the-Pros* covers the East Coast from New York to northern Virginia and Orlando and the Gulf Coast in Florida. One of the nation's largest suppliers of wedding services, the company has monthly wine and cheese parties where a variety of DJs, photographers, and videographers are presented in one place at one time. They work with hundreds of independent contractors and offer the "highest quality at the lowest prices." The charge to brides is $425 for four hours of music services, which is discounted if other services are ordered.

- *prodj.com* is the Internet source for DJs. It is linked to ultimatewedding.com and offers referrals to DJs in your area. It serves party planners, brides and grooms, and DJs and includes thousands of listings from around the world.

- *ADJA* (American DJ Association) is a national organization whose mission is information, education, and the qualification of members that ensures the highest professionalism. 888-922-ADJA. John Roberts, of the association, says, "Anyone can call themselves a DJ. It's such a fun job. But how would you feel if the DJ you hired showed up with a boom box no better than what you have?"

- *American Federation of Musicians'* New York national office will provide a list of professional musicians in any area. 212-869-1330.

- *Hank Lane Music and Productions* of New York and New Jersey is one of the largest and most prestigious suppliers of music in the Northeast, handling all aspects of music from DJs to large bands and combinations of both. They do many top celebrity weddings. Hanklane.com; 212-767-0600.

- *Musicians Network* on the West Coast is a free referral service for more than four hundred professional bands, from "Bach to Rock"; all union members. 323-993-3174.

- *Sounds of Music* on the West Coast is an internationally renowned, prestigious party band. It includes Heritage Chamber Ensembles, "the best in elegant music"—string quartets, classical guitarists, woodwind trios, etc. bc@barrycdemusic.com.

- *Wedding DJ for You* provides their own DJ services and works with five hundred other DJs. They also provide a free catalog. weddingdjforyou.com; 888-737-4333.

- *Ask a Bride* contains links to articles, information, and various wedding vendors in all fifty states. It includes a wedding bookstore linked to Barnes and Noble. wedding-world.com/illinois/musicians.html.

- *love2dj.com* is a site where you can search for a DJ in any state.

Appendix D

BUDGETING PROGRAM POSSIBILITIES—EXAMPLES				
Program possibility	#1	#2	#3	#4
Prelude				
Instruments	Guitarist	Church organist	CDs (Played by David)	DJ #1
Time allotted	3/4 hr.	As needed	3/4 hr.	As needed
Fee for prelude	$150	$150	$0	Included in total fee
Pre-processional, processional, ceremony, and recessional				
Instruments	CDs	Church organist Add soloist	CDs	DJ #1
Time allotted	3/4 hr.	As needed	As needed	As needed
Fee	$0	$150	$0	Included in total fee
Subtotal for pre-reception	$150	$300	$0	Included in total fee

BUDGETING PROGRAM POSSIBILITIES—EXAMPLES

Program possibility	#1	#2	#3	#4
Interlude				
Instruments	(No interlude)	ABC Music Co. (keyboard)	CDs	DJ #1
Time allotted		3/4 hr.	3/4 hr.	3/4 hr.
Fee for interlude	$0	$150	$0	Included in total fee
Reception				
Instruments	CDs New CDs: $75 Player and speakers: $225	ABC Music/full six-piece band	DJ #2	DJ #1, (dancers, vocalists, light show, emcee)
Time allotted	—	4 hrs.	4 hrs.	4 hrs.
Fee for reception	$300	$3,500 + $350 Tip	$750	$3,000
Subtotal for pre-reception	$150	$300	$0	Included in total fee
Total	$450	$4,300	$750	$3,000

Gloria Sklerov, a professional songwriter for more than twenty-five years and recipient of numerous BMI Awards, has been nominated for five Emmy Awards, winning two for songs featured in wedding scenes for *The Guiding Light* and *Another World*. Her work has been consistently used for character themes and featured performances in these popular shows, giving her music a widely based audience of fans and followers among daytime television viewers. Her songs have been performed worldwide in motion pictures and on television and recorded by such superstars as Frank Sinatra, Cher, Dionne Warwick, Peggy Lee, and Kenny Rogers.

Anne Murray's release of Gloria's song "I Just Fall in Love Again," a perennial wedding favorite, was recognized as Billboard's Number One Country Song of the Year in 1980, adding to the long list of Gloria's successes.

Barbara Rothstein, after practicing law for a number of years, turned to songwriting professionally in 1983. Her songs have been recorded and performed by Bobby Womack, Lisa Fisher, Melba Moore, Carl Anderson, Kathie Lee Gifford, and many others, including international artists in Europe and Japan. Many of her songs have been featured in film and on TV as well.